Isaac Mayer Wise

Judaism and Christianity

Their Agreements and Disagreements

Isaac Mayer Wise

Judaism and Christianity
Their Agreements and Disagreements

ISBN/EAN: 9783337166472

Printed in Europe, USA, Canada, Australia, Japan

Cover: Foto ©ninafisch / pixelio.de

More available books at **www.hansebooks.com**

JUDAISM AND CHRISTIANITY,

THEIR AGREEMENTS AND DISAGREEMENTS.

A Series of Friday Evening Lectures, Delivered at the Plum Street Temple, Cincinnati, Ohio,

BY THE

REV. DR. ISAAC M. WISE.

CINCINNATI:
BLOCH & CO., PUBLISHERS.
1883.

JUDAISM AND CHRISTIANITY.

THEIR AGREEMENTS AND DISAGREEMENTS.

I.
AGREEMENTS.

SAMUEL SHARSA laid down the maxim: האמת מי שלא ישיג אינו מאמין ומי שישיג מאמין—"The truth is, that he who reasons not does not believe; only he who reasons believes." This appears to be true, if we distinguish correctly between superstition and that faith which roots in conviction. Only that settled conviction can be called true belief which necessitates the mind to acknowledge the identity of its ideas with the objects in reality, as Moses Maimonides defines it. Therefore, the true religious belief, commonly called faith, must rest upon that conviction that our ideas of the objects of religion, like God, Providence, immortality, etc., are truthful representations of those objects in reality. This state of the mind can be reached by the reasoning process only.

This is the standpoint, ladies and gentlemen, which prompts us to reason on the religious beliefs which we or others may entertain. It was laid down not only by Moses Maimonides, at the very door of his rabbinical code, and by all his successors and expounders, but also before him by Bachia ben Joseph Ibn Bakoda, the very pious and orthodox author of the *Chobath Hal-lebaboth;* by Saadia the Gaon, in his *Emunoth V'adeoth;* nay, by the Prophets and by Moses, who said, "Thou hast been shown to *know* that Jehovah is God, there is none besides him;" also "*And* thou shalt *know* this day, and *reflect* in thy heart that Jehovah is God; in heaven above and on earth below there is none besides him."

This impresses us with the solemn lesson: Fear not the progress of science, dread not the discoveries of philosophy, be not terrified even by the necessity of advancing through error to truth, for truth is deathless, as God said to Moses, "This is my name forever, and this is my memorial from generation to generation;" and truth only can be the mother of true religion, while falsehood and fiction, however useful they may appear for the time being, are invariably the progenitors of degrading superstition and fanaticism. Be not alarmed if cherished beliefs examined under the light of free thought appear untenable, for there is no salvation in self-delusion, as there is none in the *Fata Morgana* for the traveler in the wilderness. Truth redeems. Truth is the prince of peace. We seek truth. If priests maintain salvation comes by faith, the uninquired and thoughtless faith, the belief in dogmas, because they are absurd, they can not prove it, as none has returned from the realms of eternity to furnish them with the evidence. It is demonstrable, however, that truth redeems, it is demonstrable by the peace and good-will, the prosperity and happiness which it brings to man on earth.

It is from this standpoint and with these lessons before our eyes that we open this evening a course of Friday evening lectures on "Judaism and Christianity; Their Agreements and Disagreements," with the intention of discussing these points thoroughly, in as far as we are capable of doing them justice, although to the best of our knowledge no Jewish lecturer has as yet ventured to discuss these topics publicly and under the light of free and independent thought. And why not? In the first place the Jews were not permitted to criticise Christianity or even to defend and expound publicly their own beliefs. Those who ventured to speak like Rabbi Lipman, the author of the *Sepher Nitzachon*, were slain or maltreated. The books were burned or stored away in some monastery where none could find them. Any passage found in any Jewish book in the least offensive to the priestly taste was eradicated by the censor, or even by the Jews themselves who feared the wrath of their neighbors. Nor were the Christians permitted to speak. Heretics and schismatics were burned by the thousands, and many more were crushed or suffocated in dismal dungeons. Giardano Bruno was not the last victim of fanaticism. He was brought to the stake and burned as an obstinate heretic in Rome, February 17, 1600, and Giardano Bruno was an independent reasoner. Nor did John Calvin do much better in Geneva in persecuting Castellio and Jerome Bolsec with hundreds and thousands of others whom he called libertines because they would not subscribe to all his doctrines; and having Servetus burned, October 27, 1553, as an incorrigible heretic. So free thought and free speech had been suppressed for fifteen long centuries, and they are yet under the ban of ostracism and under the rod of persecution in all countries except this and France. No wonder, then, that the Jew kept silent when the Christian was not permitted to speak. Nor was it advisable for the Jew to speak overly loud of his opinions among Jews, if they were of the non-conforming kind. Those who burned the books of Maimonides and raged furiously against the study of philosophy, or those who drove Uriel Acosta to suicide and excommunicated Baruch Spinoza, or those who denounced and cursed Moses Mendelssohn and his disciples, as in our very days many of these so-called reformers were hated, persecuted and denounced by their bigoted co-religionists, did certainly not encourage free thought and free speech. And so the Jew was silent, although his silence was misconstrued to the effect that Judaism had no apology for its doctrines and no arguments against its opponents.

Thank Heaven we are in America, and in Cincinnati, where free thought and free speech are the birthright of every law-abiding person. Speech and arguments govern the community, and personal liberty is esteemed as man's most precious boon. Thank Heaven that we live in an age and a country in which bigotry and fanaticism are subjected to the scepter of justice and reason, and have learned the art of moderation. Now and here, it is possible to discuss fairly any important subject, and none is more important than religion, which is after all the motive power of individual volitions, and the character of the generality. Now and here it is proper to compare and review Judaism and Christianity, their agreements and disagreements, at the electric light of reason; to criticise and expose errors with the apparatus of logic; to praise and recommend, whatever may be found praiseworthy and recommendable, without prejudice or fanaticism; to reconcile and unite, wherever conciliation is admissible and unification possible; to attack error and advance truth without malice, scorn or any unnecessary offense; to contribute a man's share to the dominion of peace and good will by a mutual better understanding of our intentions, aims and objects.

Whoever is afraid of the two-edged sword of truth and the cold steel of logic, is not expected to listen to these lectures. We say the two-edged sword, and mean what we say; for we will have to cut into both Judaism and Christianity, as there are old sores in each system which must be cut, now or later, and will be cut and healed by the world's steady progress, whether we recognize them or not. Whatever can not stand the rigid application of reason is doomed to perish. Whatever is in the way of the unity and fraternity of the human family will be overthrown. Whatever is unkind, uncharitable, ungenerous, intolerant, illiberal or unfree can not last much longer in our country. There can be no harm in exposing any elements of this kind at once and radically. Whoever can stand this process of purification is respectfully invited to aid and assist us in our search for truth. The audience is respectfully requested to excuse this lengthy preface. We go now to our subject.

It would be in its place here to give definitions of Judaism and Christianity, and I would gladly do so if anybody could define those generic terms to the satisfaction of the majority of their votaries. That which is in a continuous state of evolution can not be fixed or limited by any definition. Judaism always was in a state of evolution, as must be evident to any observer of large periods thereof. The Judaism from and after Moses was not the same as the Judaism from and after Samuel and David; nor was the Judaism of the first Hebrew Commonwealth identical with that of the second Commonwealth; so before and after the close of the Talmud; before and after the casuists had written; before and after the Spanish school, and so on to our days, Judaism changed.

The same precisely is the case with Christianity. From and after Jesus and the original Apostles; from and after Paul of Tarsus; from and after John the Evangelist; from and after the Council of Nice, the establishment of the Roman and Greek Churches; from and after the Councils and scholasts of the Middle Ages; from and after the Reformation—and so on to our days, Christianity changed and changes yet, so that every now and then a new sect springs into existence. You can not define that which admits of no definition, to cover the whole subject. At this very moment, take the past out of the consideration, it is impossible to furnish an adequate definition of either Judaism or Christianity. You send down to Longworth Street, where a small congregation of Russian orthodox Jews meet, and ask of that body, as of our friends over yonder in Lodge Street, a definition of Judaism. They let you have it to the best of their knowledge, and you read it to any of our temple congregations here, or in St. Louis, Chicago or New York, or elsewhere, and you will be frankly told that is not Judaism. Go across the street to the Roman Catholic prelate, or there to the Unitarian pastor; ask our German pastors, and then our Puritian preachers, to define Christianity for you; then compare notes, and you will find that none has given you an exact definition of Christianity, because none could do it to the satisfaction of all. There must be something wrong in all those systems, something not in harmony with reason and logic, or else the definitions must be identical, as every scientist could tell what is geometry, what is chemistry, what is physics, and so on with all the sciences. Therefore, I will not now define what is Judaism or what is Christianity. I must first investigate the elements essential to either, and then define.

In some of those essential elements Judaism and Christianity agree, are almost identical; in others, however, they differ. We will review first the " agreements," as one of my excellent friends once advised me. He said: " If you should ever feel compelled to quarrel with any neighbor about some disputed point, begin with the attempt of ascertaining in what points you agree; that matter settled, then speak of the disputed point, and in nine cases out of ten you will be astonished to discover that you did not essentially disagree at all." Let us discuss the " agreements " first.

Jew, Christian and Mohammedan agree in the belief in the existence of one God, who is the Author, Preserver and sole Sovereign of the universe, with its uncountable millions of individual beings, the Lord and Father of man and all other intelligent beings, if such exist besides man, the Eternal, Invisible, Almighty and Omnipresent, of whom Goethe has Faust, in his frivolity, sing—

" Who dares express Him?
And who confess Him,
Saying, 1 do believe?
A man's heart bearing,
What man has the daring
To say: I acknowledge him
The All-enfolder,
The All-upholder?"

Before Him, who is the mystery of mysteries, and yet the clearest of all revelations reaching the human mind, the most distant and the nearest, most cogitable and unknowable, before Him, Jew, Christian and Mohammedan stand in awe, feel His presence, think of His greatness, praise, worship and glorify His holy name.

Thus much has been gained in the world's progress, that all civilized nations believe in the living God of Israel. The atheist is neither Jew, Christian nor Mohammedan. The difference between these three faiths is not in the substance of this doctrine; it is in its accidents. They differ in definitions. The trinitarian believes not in three Gods; his definition of the one God distinguishes his faith from that of other monotheists, and makes him intolerant toward them. Not what God is supposed to have revealed of himself, but what man has added, is the element of disturbance. As in time of yore the Prophet exclaimed: " Have we not all one Father; hath not one God created us?" we may repeat now, and admonish all the children of the civilized nations in the words of another prophet: " Peace, peace to him who is nigh and to him who is far off, saith Jehovah, and 1 will heal him."

Again, Jew, Christian and Mohammedan believe alike that this physical world is of God's creation. He preceded it; He designed and executed; He made and shaped it.

" He said—and it was;
He commanded—and there it stood."

The spirit is the substance of all being, and preceded it; the spirit only is from eternity to eternity; the spirit is absolute, and all material things are not, because their existence is relative, subject to perpetual change; they are and are not; they become and perish. Thus all of them agree upon the substantiality and omnipotence of the spirit, the accidentality and inferiority of matter, which is the creature and the servant of the Most High. Therefore, they also agree that God's power and wisdom pervade and govern all things in this immense universe. God's providence extends over all his creatures, the hosts on high, the sun and stars, and the hosts below, man and beast, elephant or worm, cedar or fungus, all, all of them are objects of his care, provided for and controlled by his wisdom and power. The spirit reigns and matter obeys. The Mohammedan may incline more to fatalism than some of us do; not, indeed, by Mohammed's teachings, but in consequence of his expounders; still all maintain and all profess "Jehovah reigneth forever and aye," as did redeemed Israel at the Red Sea.

Furthermore, Jew, Christian and Mohammedan believe alike in the spirit of man being substance of the divine substance, with qualities of the eternal spirit, and, therefore, immortal like the deathless source from which it flows and in which it exists in time and eternity, consciously or unconsciously, in the purity of holiness or the brutality of sensual and carnal depravity, at the height of self-consciousness and the blissful memory of goodness, or the twilight idiocy and the painful recollections of self-inflicted evil. So the water remains the same crystal fluid as it is in the spring in the rock, although it may, mixed with the mire, become Ohio or Mississippi water, it is water still. The element (the substance) changes not. All of them believe in the essence and immortality of the soul, in this or that form, and in some kind of reward and punishment, however uncharitably they may exclude one another from the kingdom of heaven, and expel the children from the Father's house, in consequence of human deductions and unreasoning fanaticism; yet all believe the same fundamental doctrine as a characteristic of human nature.

Again, Jew, Christian and Mohammedan do verily believe that God revealed himself or his will to Abraham and Moses, to and through the prophets and bards of Israel; all believe in the revelation on Mount Sinai, in this or that form, so explained or otherwise, and all believe more or less in miracles, in the natural or supernatural form, and all point to them as a species of evidence upon which their respective faith rests. Therefore the question arises, If they thus agree, why do they thus disagree? If their beliefs are so much alike in the main, why do they denounce, hate, persecute and even abhor one another, as history tells they did and partly do now? Why should they not look first and foremost upon those main points, in which they agree, and admonish one another to peace and good will, and address to each other the prophetical words, " Go ye, and let us ascend the mountain of Jehovah"? It is all on account of the unfortunate " Disagreements," which we propose to discuss in subsequent lectures. They are the cause of the misery, the numerous woes, the tears and blood, the ugly stains in the history of civilization. As to the points of agreement and the religion based upon them, King David has provided us (Psalms xv.) with a splendid catechism, which, we think, suffices to all good men:

"O Jehovah, who shall dwell in thy tent, who shall abide in thy holy mountain?

"He that walketh uprightly, worketh righteousness and speaketh the truth in his heart; that uttereth no calumny with his tongue, doeth no evil to his neighbor, and bringeth no reproach on his fellow-man, in whose eyes the despicable is despised; he who honoreth those who fear Jehovah, and having sworn even to his injury, changeth not; that giveth not his money for usury, and taketh no bribe against the innocent.

"He that doeth these things shall not be moved to eternity."

Thank you, King David, for this universal catechism. Whereas, neither rabbi, nor priest, nor dervish can improve it, we stop here and keep our "Disagreements" for another lecture.

II.

INSPIRATION, PROPHECY AND REVELATION.

THE Bible is a great book, although many critics say it is not. The world does not agree with them. The world changes and we change with it, still the world did not change in this one point, as it yet maintains that the Bible is a great book. *Vox populi, vox Dei* is in Hebrew *KoL HAMMON KE-KOL SHADDAI, and Cicero's argument, based on the common consent of all nations (*Argumentum a consensu gentium*), must not be taken too lightly, especially not by a jurist, for all men know more than any one man; and when we speak of human reason we mean the reason of humanity, or, at least, of that portion thereof that is capable of reasoning.

· Why does the world ascribe so much importance to that collection of books called the Bible? Because one portion thereof is a direct revelation from on high, it is maintained, a momentary crevice in heaven's impenetrable dome, through which mortals beheld the glory of the Majesty on high; and another portion was written down by men, divinely inspired, for truth, righteousness, the salvation and happiness of man. How do you know that this is so? reason asks the believing multitude. By the internal evidence which the book offers is one answer; by the uninterrupted traditions and the common consent of the civilized world is the other. The book offers the most sublime lessons, most impressively formulated, on the nature and will of God, the duty, dignity and hope of man, and the efficient and final causes of the universe and the cosmos therein, while similar books of other nations of antiquity contain but grains of the universal truth under a vast heap of chaff rejected by human reason. They represent small creeks, and the Bible is the broad stream of those lessons of salvation which organize, civilize, humanize and sanctify the human family. This is its internal evidence. The Hebrews, as far as their history reaches, together with the Christian and Mohammedan Scriptures and nations from their respective beginnings to this date testify to the holiness and divinity of the Bible, and have established and conduct society on the principles and laws contained in that book, because being of divine origin, they are considered supreme and universal, and base the duties and hopes of the indi-

---

* קול המון כקול שדי

vidual man on those very lessons. This is the historical evidence. Excepting the few voices of skeptics and unbelievers which reach us from the past, up to the very door of the nineteenth century, the premises are correct, the argument is acceptable and the evidence conclusive in as far as circumstantial evidence suffices to establish a fact.

Here, however, reason interposes a very important objection, which is this: The supremacy and dignity of your holy books rest upon the allegations of inspiration, prophecy and revelation. These appear to be not only supersensual but even supernatural manifestations, which no man whose knowledge is only sensual and natural in its foundations can establish. We divide the question and give the following two answers:

The knowledge which we derive by our corporeal senses is the smallest fraction of man's actual knowledge. There is in man a sentient, thinking and productive principle which penetrates far beyond the sphere of the senses. Not only all our purely religious, ethical and metaphysical speculations and conceptions, but also the sciences, or rather that principal portion thereof which constructs science of the detached facts of our sensual experience and experiments are absolutely supersensual. As absurd as it is for any man of sound sense to maintain that he can believe nothing which he could not see, *i. e.*, not perceive with his senses and grasp with his animal intellect, equally unphilosophical is the allegation that supersensual manifestations can not be proved by the logical process. No sensible man doubts that the sun is a fixed star around which the earth, with the other planets and moons of the system, revolve, whatever the Book of Joshua may assert to the contrary, and yet Copernicus, Keppler, Galileo and Newton did not construct the evidence in support of that supersensual fact from sensual perceptions and observations. And yet nine-tenths of all men know and believe this fact by tradition only, by the *argumentum a consensu gentium*—the common consent of the nations—precisely in the same manner as they know that the Bible is a divine book. Sensualism as a philosophical basis is but one side, and the lower one only, of the foundation of truth.

Revelation, however one might explain it, signifying a supernatural communication to man coming from God directly or indirectly by his angels or otherwise, how could man, reasoning logically, arrive at the evidence in support of such a manifestation? We say that materialism, realism and positivism; also Spinozism, are obliged to take the supernatural for granted, although they can neither prove nor disprove it; for they can not close their eyes to the conscience and consciousness of man, reason, freedom, ideality, moral feeling and æsthetical taste, all of which are inexplicable by all the laws, hypotheses and theories of and concerning matter and force;

hence they are supernatural facts with all of them, and facts they are, notwithstanding those gentlemen's inability to explain or prove them. They must admit that revelation is only one more supernatural fact in addition to many others which they can not explain, prove or disprove.

The theist, however, all those who start from the premises concerning God, man and their mutual relation, which we have laid down in the first lecture of this series, can not deny the possibility, and is necessitated by reasoning from analogy to admit the spiritual *raport* between God and man. Here you stand in this physical world. Each considers himself a person, a being complete and independent, of distinct and individual existence. And yet your relation to this physical nature with all its elements and forces is constant and continuous. With a thousand invisible threads you are tied to this physical world at large, and each is a channel to conduct into you the gifts of nature which you continually reciprocate. You affect and are affected without rest or pause, you are in this material nature a mere part thereof and in constant *raport* with it, although you appear to be a complete and independent individual. Well, then, you who believe in the existence of the one and eternal God, who is omnipotent and omnipresent; you who believe in the spirit of man and its Godlike qualities, by what process of reasoning could you doubt the continuous spiritual *raport* of the individual spirit with the universal spirit, if you must admit the perpetual *raport* of individualized and cosmic matter, when the one process is evidently as supernatural as the other? You see, appealing to reason, there is no cause why the supernatural manifestations of inspiration, prophecy and revelation should not be accepted as facts. Therefore, the vast majority of men could and did accept them, and the most eminent philosophers of all past centuries, Plato, Aristotle included, could expound and advocate them. "I am no better than my ancestors."

We have now arrived at the main object of this lecture, viz: the consideration of these three terms: Inspiration, prophecy and revelation, and herewith we have also arrived at the first point of disagreement in Judaism and Christianity.

Inspiration signifies to bring in spirit, viz: into any person by an outward agency, and thus increase quantitatively the spirit of that person, giving him more spirit. In this form, however, it is a New Testament idea, where the Holy Ghost is supposed to have come down in a materialized form, as a dove, upon Jesus after his baptism, or in the shape of fiery tongues, upon the apostle on the Day of Pentecost. The ancient Hebrews did not connect the spirit with the idea of quantity. Therefore, they had no word for inspiration, as they had no idea of conducting spirit into a man, as heat, magnetism or electricity might be conducted into him. Nor is the expression Holy Ghost (Hebrew *Ruach hac-Kodesh*) found anywhere in the Old Testament; it is New Hebraic, and was coined by the Rabbis, perhaps in imitation of the terms used by the early Christians. The Biblical idea as worded by the later prophets especially, " And there was upon me the hand (or power) of God;" "There was upon me the spirit of God;" "Then the spirit lifted me up," and similar phrases express the idea that the spirit of the favored man or woman was by a divine influence elevated, heightened, its latent energies developed into actuality, by the mediation of a burning bush in the case of Moses, by a vision of the throne of glory in the cases of Isaiah and Ezekiel, and other occurrences in the cases of other prophetical or inspired men. Here is the idea of quality rather than of quantity, the spirit of man possesses the latent qualities or capacities to be roused to a state of inspiration by a combination of outward circumstances, which God may have produced directly or indirectly. If that state of inspiration was durable for any length of time in any person, or even on any place which exercised such an inspiring influence, it was described, also by post-biblical authorities as the SHĔKĪNAH dwelling, resting or abiding upon that person or place. Also this term and phrase were coined by the Rabbis, and do not occur in the Old Testament, and still later God himself was called the Shekinah, as he was called *Shamayim*, "Heaven," *Ham-mokom*, " the place," or also *Rachmana*, " Love or the Merciful."

. You see, the Christian idea of inspiration is altogether supernatural, while the Jewish idea is natural and rational. The marvelous element in it is limited to the inborn capacities of the favored person and the combination of outward circumstances as the agency to unfold the potential to actual energies. This is, perhaps, the cause of the entirely different views held by Jews and Christians concerning the divinity of the Bible, which we will discuss some other time. Here we will only remark that all ancient philosophers, Plato and Aristotle, the Arabian, Jewish and Christian metaphysicians of the Middle Ages accepted inspiration as a fact, natural or supernatural, which they attempted to analyze and explain psychologically. Among Jews it was, especially Saadia, Abraham Ibn Daud, Moses Maimonides, with his numerous expounders and followers, who adhered to the natural aspect of inspiration, and they succeeded in impressing it upon Judaism. Those worthies had accepted the idea of Rabbi Joshua ben Chananiah, who in his controversy with Rabbi Eliezer ben Hyrcan in the Academy of Jamnia (end of the first Christian century) declared, and the whole College agreed with him, that miracles prove nothing, and " We pay no attention to the *Bath-kol*;" and this *Bath-kol* was in form and essence identical with the Christian idea of inspiration, both being supernatural and concrete in their manifestations. Rabbi Eliezer, who adhered to supernaturalism, was excommunicated by the College, although he was the brother-in-law of Rabban Gamaliel, then Prince and Patriarch in Israel. The principle thus illustrated was accepted by Rabbi Akiba, who with three of his cotemporaries went into Gnostic speculations and practices to obtain knowledge by inspiration, and at last came to the conclusion, "Thy doings (thine own) bring thee nearer (to the Deity), and thy doings remove thee (from Him);" which is to say that thy wisdom, righteousness and holiness achieve for thee that victory over man's ignorance and wickedness which thou seekest in that state of inspiration.

The subjective evidence of divine inspiration is the irresistible longing to do some great deed or to utter some important truth in the name of God and for the benefit and blessing of man, especially when mankind stands in need of such deeds or such utterances; then those needs are the outer circumstances which attract and captivate the favored man's attention, engage and actuate his mind, and finally become to him the cause of inspiration, if by nature he is gifted with superior fancy, his intelligence and ethical character are correspondingly developed and perfected, and his mind is directed to the sublime and divine, the true and the good. The impulse to perform valorous deeds for the salvation of man in their mundane affairs, as recorded of Samson, or of Gideon, Jephthah and David mark the lowest degree of inspiration, an inspiration manifested in valorous deeds. A second and higher degree of inspiration manifests itself by the sacred poet's inner desire to sing the praise of the Almighty, to advance and adore truth and righteousness, to pour forth in the form of the beautiful and sublime the lyric strains of the soul, and sing of eternal truth and adoration, devotion, resignation, hope and thanksgiving, as in the song of Moses, at the Red Sea, the song of Deborah, the Psalms of David, Asaph, Jeduthun, the Sons of Korah, the Proverbs of Solomon, the Philosophism of Job and other productions of the kind.

The next higher degree of inspiration, according to Jewish conception, is the lowest degree of prophecy, which, like the productions of prophecy, is again divided in various degrees, one above the other, up to Moses, who was THE prophet emphatically, as Maimonides maintains, while all other prophets are only called so on account of the homonymy of the term. This opinion of Maimonides is based upon various ancient maxims recorded in the Talmud, especially the following: " All the prophets received their inspiration from Mount Sinai." " None of the prophets and prophetesses added to the laws of Moses or abrogated any one thereof." " Moses saw (Deity and truth) by the clearest reflector; the prophets saw by a dim reflector." You may add thereto the statements of Scriptures (Numb. xii,

5–8; Deuteronomy xxxiii. 10–12; Isaiah lv. 10–12) upon which Jesus based his allegation, that he had not come to abolish, but to fulfill the Law, not a title or iota of which should fall to the ground; simply because Moses was THE prophet in the estimation of all his prophetical successors.

Here we have arrived at another point of disagreement in Judaism and Christianity, viz : in the definition of the ideas : What constitutes a prophet? what must a man do to deserve the acknowledgment of man as a divinely inspired messenger? what is the nature, the psychology of prophecy? Christianity starting with inspiration from the supernatural standpoint must consistently maintain that the prophet is the divinely commissioned man to a certain religious end, who predicts future events and works miracles. Therefore, both Jesus and his original apostles, also Paul, according to statements of the Acts of the Apostles, and a number of primitive Christians prophesied and wrought miracles. A similar idea is also expressed in the *Talmud Yerushalmi*, where the old maxim, "The wise man is superior to the prophet," is illustrated by a king sending to his subjects two commissioners, one his servant and the other his intimate friend. The document given to the former tells the king's subjects that his commissioner will prove them his identity by the royal insignia which he carries (prediction and miracles in the case of the prophet). The document given to the intimate friend (the savan) recommends him to the king's subjects on the man's own merits, which can be demonstrated to all men. Still it can not be denied that almost all the prophets whose literary productions we possess wrought no miracles, and most of their predictions, if not all of them, point to events so near their respective days, or at least they might be so understood, that prophesying appears to have been no criterion for the genuine prophet. Therefore, we think it has been set down by Moses Maimonides in the Rabbinical Code (*Yesodei hat-Thorah*, chapters viii. and x., twice translated into English), hence not as his private opinion, but as the traditional doctrine of the Hebrews; that neither miracles nor predictions prove the prophet; that we do not believe in Moses because he did perform miracles; and that these were not the criteria of any prophet after him. It will be necessary to discuss and understand this "disagreement" and its fundamental principles. Therefore, ladies and gentlemen, I am sorry, and beg your pardon, that I could not fully keep my promise this evening to discuss inspiration, prophecy and revelation. as I do not believe I am entitled any longer to the privilege of addressing you, and can only invite you to call again next Friday evening, if you wish to hear the rest of this discourse, which we now conclude with the words of Elihu in the Book of Job, "Verily it is the spirit in the human being and the breath of the Almighty which giveth them intelligence."

III.

PROPHECY, REVELATION AND THE BIBLE.

The prophet, the man of God, of whom we read in Scriptures, was neither the soothsayer, such as figures in the Egyptian processions and the Grecian oracles; nor the legerdemainist of Arabia and India, who mumbled magic spells and performed marvelous tricks; he had nothing in common with the exorcist and thaumaturgist of other days, and had no dealings with Satan and his host of evil spirits; nor was he of the same kind with the mystics and ascetics who dwelt in sylvan retreats, in dark caves or obscure grottoes fasting, praying and divining; he was entirely unlike the saints, monks and dervishes of later days; he was a man and a patriot, the *Ish-Elohim*, "the man of God," concerning whom it was believed, " Whatever he speaketh will surely come to pass " (I. Samuel ix. 6), to whom people went " To inquire of God " (*Ibid.*), for in olden days the time of extreme simplicity, the *Nabi* " prophet " was also called *ha-Roeh*, " the seer," and was supposed to unravel mysteries also for private individuals. (*Ibid.*) This, however, was only exceptionally the case. The character and office of the prophet in Israel was that of the sublime and patriotic statesman with the broad, vast and generous conceptions, who in the name of God and his law, spoke to the people or its leaders and teachers words of righteousness, admonitions of piety, lessons of wisdom, accompanied by menaces of dire punishment to the disobedient and rebellious, and promises of the divine favor to the righteous and veracious, the patriotic and just, the humane and generous benefactors of man. These are the main contents of all predictions recorded in the Book, as made by the prophets, and on this principle only did they prophesy future events, as means, not as ends, of their mission. The legends of miracles are very few and far apart, after Moses and Joshua, Elijah and Elisha, Daniel and his very pious friends, so that the most remarkable prophets, Isaiah, Jeremiah, Ezekiel and the twelve Minor Prophets, with only one exception, wrought no miracles at all, and the one or two supposed miracles wrought by Isaiah (II. Kings xx. 7, 11) must have been strictly private. Moses had already cautioned his people not to attach any importance to predictions or miracles, where they are intended to contradict first principles, the dicta of reason (Deuter. xiii. 2-6; xviii. 20-22); therefore, Jewish theologians attached less importance to predictions and miracles than to the dicta of reason and the plain teachings of the Bible.

The Hebrew term *Nabi*, " prophet " is derived from *Naba* (see Fuerst), "to spout, to pour forth," and signifies a man who pours forth fluent speech, an eloquent orator. The term is used in Scriptures for both the true and the false prophet, the prophet of Jehovah or of Baal and Astarte. The oldest Aramaic version extant, ascribed to Jonathan ben Uziel in the century B. C., renders (I. Samuel x. 5) the term *Chebel Nebiim* (a band of prophets) by *Siath Saphria*, " A band of Scribes " or perhaps " orators," which affords an insight into the opinion of the ancient Hebrews concerning the prophet. He was the popular orator, the mouthpiece of truth and righteousness, the personified free press and free speech in Israel, under the special protection of God and the Law. The form changed, the fundamental idea remains, and is fundamental yet in the progress of civilization and the enlightenment of nations.

In the Mosaic dispensation the head of the republic was to be a prophet, or rather the principle one of his age (compare Exodus xxiii. 20-23 with Deuter. xviii. 15-22), and he was the only human being in the theocracy concerning whom the Law commands, " Ye shall hearken to him," which distinction was bestowed on neither priest nor prince. Therefore, all heads of the Hebrew Republic down to King Saul were called prophets by posterity, as the heroic Deborah, being at the head of the theocracy is given the title in Scriptures, " And Deborah was a prophetical woman;" and the books narrating their exploits were placed in that division of the Bible which is called the Former Prophets. After the revolution under Samuel, when Israel rejected the Mosaic theocracy, and established the kingdom, the king, of course, was at the head of the new theocracy, and he also, as in the case of Saul, David and Solomon, was supposed to be a prophet. Still the actual prophet remained the most important and most influential man in the State, before whom kings and high-priests bowed down with reverence, not merely because they were the men of God, but because they were the men of the people, the advocates of Law, and the protectors of the nation's rights and liberties, the guardians of truth and righteousness, with which, and for which, they were inspired. One thousand years of history elapsed between Moses and Malachi, and during all that time the prophetical voice resounded with might. With the courage of the lion they rebuked kings and warriors, priests and princes, the nation and her wicked men; and yet only two prophets, two in one thousand years, were slain in

Judea, and in Israel, but once the wicked and idolatrous Ahab and Jezebel persecuted and slew them. So it appears that also the most wicked in Israel stood in veneration and awe before the messengers of the Most High, announcing to them the oracles of the Living God. The prophet was a unique institution found among the ancient Hebrews only.

Who and what were those mental colossuses, that their persons and their oracles were so sacred to their cotemporaries and to posterity? Moses Maimonides answered this question most naturally. In harmony with the philosophy of his age, as far as he could indorse it, and basing upon passages of the Bible and rabbinical writings, he gives us the psychology of the prophet. He maintains that, like every other genius, the prophet is born, as it is supposed that God said to Jeremiah (i. 5), for a genius he is in the noblest sense of the term. His capacities are inborn, his abilities are acquired by training, his oracles are the free gift of God, in correspondence with his natural capacities and acquired abilities, which enable the individual spirit to stand in closer communion with the universal spirit than other mortals can, and thus conceive verities and foresee events unknown to the ordinary mind. His natural capacities are, besides courage and predictive power, a sound, normal and harmonious organism. In the first place the imaginative power which quickly turns abstract ideas into living, moving and plastic entities, standing in bold relief, as it were, before the mind's eye, acting and speaking in the form of reality, so that the subjective becomes objective, and the person sees and hears without that which actually occurs within himself. This organon to perceive conceptions is the common criterion of genius, and depends for its material on two points, the acquired abilities and the outer circumstances. With the prophet, Maimonides maintains that the acquired abilities must be of the highest intellectual and moral grades. His reasoning capacities must be developed by study and training, by science and reflection to a clear and energetic reasoning power, so that the association of ideas, the classification of the homogeneous, and the process of judgment be rapid and correct, so much so that he himself can not observe the rapid progress from the premises or antecedents to the conclusions. His moral capacities must be ennobled and invigorated by steady exercise in the good and the true, so that his animal instincts and passions be perfectly subservient to reason, and he can only wish and love, think and feel the good and the true, and all that is wicked, false, low or mean become to him unnatural and repulsive. If thus fancy, reason and morals are harmoniously developed in a man who has overcome his worldly ambitions, the vulgar strivings, longings and yearnings of the common man, and his soul is stimulated by the one great desire for truth and righteousness, the sublime knowledge of God and His government, the elevation and happiness of man ; he is preparing to become a prophet, and may become one, if the outer circumstances do not disturb him in his work of spiritual elevation, and the concurrence of events do not turn his mind in other directions. So the genius becomes a prophet after he has risen gradually from the sphere of pure imagination to the temple of moral grandeur, to the sunny height of sublime reason, to the loftiest problems of the human mind, the mysteries of existence and that mystery of mysteries which is to lead man to perfection and happiness. So the prophet is educated. This is the analysis of his soul according to Moses Maimonides, whose thoughts are well grounded upon Sacred Scriptures and the traditions of Israel. Whether in that exalted state of mind man will receive any message from on high, or in our modern phraseology will conceive original ideas on the truths which he seeks and the salvation he desires to bring to man, depends on the will of God and the combination of outer circumstances.

Did such men ever exist? If they did, they will remain forever the glory of the human family. Poor creatures as we are, ingulfed in this material world, ever troubled and vexed by a thousand small necessities, weighed down by prodigal instincts and creeping along like snails upon the mire of accumulated passions, we can hardly think that such men ever existed, such giant natures, such seraphic minds. Among us one has the fancy, another the reason, and alas ! another again the moral greatness ; one has the partial means and another the untoward desire to rise and ascend the mountain of God ; and all, all of us appear to have become fractional men with some excellencies and many deficiencies.

We can, perhaps, no longer imagine or even think the perfect man in the fulness of his manhood and his nearness to the Eternal Deity. And yet, according to the beliefs and traditions of Israel there were such men, and those men were the prophets; and those prophets have bequeathed us the grand legacy of the prophetical books contained in the Bible. Therefore, those books are so much greater and holier than other books as their authors were superior to all others known to fame. Their nearness to the Eternal Deity is the objective evidence of the truth of prophecy. There exists no better species of evidence in the world. The sons of the house must know the father's will. Now look upon the ancient Hebrew prophet, contemplate him from the standpoint of reason, scrutinize him with the skeptic's critical eye, then compare him with all persons known to you personally or by tradition ; and I think you will agree with me that the prophet was a man as unique and distinguished as are the prophetical Scriptures among all other literary productions. And yet he was only man and no more—a man with faults and deficiencies, mortal like others ; and there was evidently nothing so supernatural about him, that it is not in perfect harmony with human reason. The only difficulty we might experience in identifying the true prophet with the natural man is in our false conceptions of man, his ability and perfectibility.

And yet neither the inspired bard nor the wisest of all teachers; neither the holy seer nor the greatest of all prophets is looked upon from the Jewish standpoint as the organ of revelation. "All the prophets received their inspiration from Mount Sinai," which is to say that the prophets merely expounded and promulgated the Sinaic revelation; or there was only one revelation, which was that from Mount Sinai. All of them spake like Moses, and Moses spake like the expounder of the Sinaic revelation. It is all one spirit—one and the same contents. One God, one truth, one and the same lesson of righteousness, which, spouting from Sinai, saturate all biblical books from one end to the other. There is nothing new under the sun, not even in the Bible. Its gold coins are from the mines of Horeb, moulded and cast in different forms, but always the same metal. If the Sinaic revelation is true, the whole must be true, and requires no other evidence.

If in anywise the One and Eternal God communicated with the people of Israel through the thunders and lightnings of Sinai, then we know by the most convincing evidence that Jehovah is God; in heaven above and on earth below there is none besides him. We know that this very Jehovah is "thy Elohim," the Creator and Preserver of the world; the Leggislator, Judge and King; the Providence of the human family, and every individual thereof; the Almighty King "who brought thee out of the land of Egypt;" and that he delights in justice, freedom and righteousness, for he redeemed you from the house of bondage, to legislate for you and point out for you the path of righteousness to national prosperity and human happiness. The introductory verse to the Sinaic revelation suffices not only to silence all skepticism and to provide man with the light of Heaven, but it is also all-sufficient as the principle upon which all moral laws are based, all civilizing, humanizing and sanctifying institutions of man can be founded, and, in fact, are founded more or less, and all hopes of man can be safely rested; for all ethical conceptions and all immortality speculations derive their existence from that one verse of Scripture. If that is true, then the whole economy of the Bible, the entire code of morals, the whole fabric of government, the institution of worship, together with all the duties and hopes of man, as suggested therein, must be true, for they are all derived from this axiom, from which they rise and in which they find their evidence. Therefore some rabbis of the Talmud maintained the first two sentences of the Decalogue all Israel heard directly from the Almighty, because they contain all that is necessary for man to know and understand in order to erect upon it the entire structure of morals, religion, government and prosperity on earth, happiness and glory in eternity. The one God, the free man who communicates with the Eternal, the one intelligence and love universal and individualized, the law of righteousness as the fruit thereof, suffice as the postulate to what all men need to know to fulfill their destiny and realize their hopes in time and eternity.

Then the Sinaic revelation promulgates the categories of doctrines and laws, precepts finished and embodied in laws, categories covering the entire moral and religious sphere of man, flowing like a stream from that eternal source announced in the first sentence, the perfect system in a few words, to which nothing could be added and nothing taken away, as the law of the covenant between God and Israel, the covenant between God and man, all of which is true and unalterable, if the first sentence is true, viz: " I, Jehovah, am thy *Elohim*"; and all of which is a complex of ingenious air castles, if the first sentence is fictitious. If Israel heard the first he heard also the last, for all is included in the first and all depends on it. Therefore the economy of the Bible, looked upon from this standpoint, is the following :

All divine revelation is contained in principle in the Sinaic revelation, and all revelation has for its object the instruction of man in his duties, destiny and just expectations, to secure to him the highest good, happiness in time and eternity.

Moses, who was appointed by Providence to redeem Israel from Egyptian bondage, was also divinely appointed to organize the covenant people, to represent among men God's will and government, and he did organize it by establishing immediate and prophetic laws and institutions on the Sinaic principle with special respect to time and place, to outer circumstances and traditional habits which could not be eradicated at once, and to the moral and religious status of the then civilized portion of the human family. Every law of Moses, excepting only those which were of momentary necessity, is the embodiment of a Sinaic principle made tangible and effectual to meet emergencies or regulate affairs at that time and place, so that the principle is eternal and referable to the Sinaic revelation, while the law as such is transitory. All new revelations which Moses is supposed to have had were of an explanatory nature, to him personally, to assist him in the organization of the covenant people on the Sinaic principles. (Compare Exodus xxxiv. 27, 28; xiv. 31; xix. 5, 6, 9; xx. 18, 19, with Deuteronomy iv. 9-14, 35, 36; v. 1-5, 17-30, and parallel passages.)

The prophets after Moses were the guardians and expounders of the Sinaic revelation in the form of the laws of Moses or in such other forms as time and circumstances required. The Council of Seventy Elders and the priests were the guardians of the letter and the prophets of the spirit of the divine law. Whatever revelations they may have had or whatever miracles they are reported to have wrought were auxiliary only to protect, expound, enforce, apply and advocate the Sinaic revelation, the eternal law under the various emergencies and circumstances. This was their office, their sole function, to which they added not and from which they took nothing away. The first and the last book of the Bible is of the same spirit; every sentence of the whole collection is explanatory of the Sinaic revelation. If this is true all is true.

But here we stand before a miracle; in fact, besides the creation of the world, the greatest and most marvelous of all miracles ever conceived by the human mind. Is there, can there be any logical ground on which to accept this miracle and believe in it? Human reason revolts against the idea of miracle. Are there any rational grounds in existence to correct the human reason on this particular point?

Ladies and gentlemen, I have attempted this evening to expound the Jewish standpoint as I understood it in regard to prophecy, revelation and the Bible within the bounds of reason, except this one point of the Sinaic revelation, and on this one point I must politely beg you to grant me extension till Friday evening next, when I will make the attempt to pay also this debt.

IV.

THE JEWISH AND THE CHRISTIAN EVIDENCES OF REVELATION COMPARED.

The spirit of the age, it would appear to me, is concentrated in the one English word—emancipation. As in the political life of the civilized nations, so in all other spheres and provinces of intellectual activity the Genius of the Ninteenth Century combats the power of authority and seeks emancipation. In our country and in the political arena that combat begins with the revolution, triumphs in establishing the principle of freedom and equality, civil and religious liberty, rises gradually to the abolition of slavery, and culminates temporarily in the overthrow of bossism. The same spirit of emancipation rouses the European nations, and makes itself felt up to the very palace of the Russian autocrat, the Vatican and the Mosque of Mecca, although slower in its progress, and beset by more obstacles and impediments than in our country. Science and philosophy, art, that most slavish subject of antique models and patterns, yea, also art, commerce and all forms of industry strive to liberate themselves from authority, seek emancipation. We must be free, is the categorical imperative of our age.

The idea of revelation is identical with that of authority. Therefore, the consciousness of the time objects to it. Many intelligent, conscientious, and even religious men, believing in the self-sufficiency of human reason, reject the theory of revelation. I believe, however, that I have proved in a former lecture of this series that this theory is not contrary to reason, and is in perfect harmony with undoubted natural phenomena; to which I beg leave to add here, that in the face of empiric facts all objections of reason are unreasonable, since facts will not remodel themselves to correspond with our ideas, reason must modify its decisions to identify its ideas with the empiric facts. Well, then revelation is represented to us as an empiric fact, which is in nowise invalidated by the objections of our reason or the consciousness of our age, as the question is not whether we understand or appreciate it; the only legitimate inquiry could be, does the historical testimony presented to us warrant the belief that such an event transpired?

On the other hand it must be admitted that historical testimony only is admissible in establishing a historical fact. Let us review some of the testimony which we must reject. In consideration of what has been said before on the subject of miracles, it must be self-understood that the testimony of miracles is no evidence of revelation, because in the first place there exists no logical connection between the accident of the miracle and the substance of the revelation. If, for instance, any person would maintain that God revealed to him or her that three times three are ten, and, in proof of his divine mission, would cause the hills in our vicinity to skip liké rams, many of us might be overawed and believe, while reasoning men would say they knew not how that man performed that task and would continue in their belief that three times three are nine, as the skipping of the hills and a mathematical verity have not the least connection with one another.

Still less weighty is the narrated miracle; even if it was proved that the narrator or writer was an eye-witness. Quite a number of doubts naturally arise in the mind, and the hearer or reader is apt to ask himself questions of this kind: Was it the author's intention to report truth or fiction? Did he write to inform or to edify? If he intended to report truth, did he see and hear correctly, was he in a state of mind and in the position to comprehend well whatever he did see or hear? Did the writer not amplify and exaggerate, did he not employ figurative and symbolical language to give poetical ornamentation to common and natural events? Did he not write *post festum* from popular traditions colored by poetical fancy? These and other questions of the same nature render the written or narrated miracle unfit and untoward as testimony to establish truth.

Again, miracles must be believed, they can never appeal to reason. Each miracle requires a separate act of belief. Those who expect us to believe in revelation which is a miracle according to that supernatural standpoint, and then want us to believe another number of miracles in order to establish the fact of revelation, evidently ask too much of the reasoning man. We can more easily believe one than a dozen miracles, especially if any one suffices to prove the dominion of mind over matter, and the one, as is the case in the Sinaic revelation, conveys all the instruction to the human mind which it needs, to understand the relation between God and man, and affords him a valid standard of truth and righteousness. Nor can we, by the aid of a thousand miracles, do better than believe that one which we do believe. It does not improve the case.

The same precisely is the case with prophecy or prediction and its fulfillment. It has no logical connection whatever with the substance of any supposed revelation. If a man predicted one event or ten and more, which ally came to pass, it is no convincing criterion that every other statement of his must be undoubtedly true, or that God has selected him as an organ of revelation; and besides this the supposed predictions are subject to all the doubts raised against miracles.

The other aspect of this point is no less invalid as a proof of revelation. To maintain that any person must be, or has been, the organon of revelation, because preceding prophets predicted his coming, his life and death, is again the same thing as above, viz : to believe in many miracles where one suffices. Each of those predictions must have been a miracle. Besides, predictions are made in words which must be expounded, expounders widely differ in opinions, and evidently there exists no final authority in this case to decide those differences; hence it could at no time be said with any degree of certainty that the person who, in the opinion of one class, accidentally corresponds to those predictions, was actually the object thereof, or that not a thousand or more persons may exist hereafter to correspond as well, or even better, to those predictions. ' With all those doubts surrounding the testimony, no impartial judge could admit them as evidence to establish the fact of revelation, if it be denied on the ground of reason which rejects revelation, or on the ground of Judaism, which maintains the sufficiency of the Sinaic revelation. All this, however, does not prove that no miracles have been wrought, and no events predicted by inspired men. It is absurd to reason against facts because we can not understand them; it merely sets forth that one miracle can not be proved by others, every one of which is without proof, in fact. Therefore, we must come back to the historical evidence.

The Sinaic revelation announces itself in the sources as a fact which transpired in broad daylight before the eyes of a whole nation of men, women and children. The Book informs us, "And all the people perceived the thunders and the lightnings and the voice of the cornet and the smoking mount; the people saw, were moved, and stood afar off." Also the people said to Moses, " Speak thou unto us and we will listen, and let not (further) God speak to us, lest we die." So they also said, "This day have we seen that God speaketh to man and he liveth." Whoever reads the corresponding chapters of Exodus and Deuteronomy must feel convinced that the author thereof intended to narrate a fact of which he was an eye witness, and this fact is that all the people heard the substance of the revelation, and stood in awe before the accompanying demonstrations. There is no attempt at poetical embellishment or rhetorical ornamentation; it is fact, fact, fact which the author intended to narrate.

A whole nation saw and heard the Sinaic revelation. This is one of the main points, for this never occurred again, neither before nor after that memorable event. The witnesses of all miraculous events recorded in the Old and New Testaments were small in number, and the correctness of their perceptions and conceptions might justly be questioned, even if the reports are correct. But in this case a nation is the witness, a nation which by preceding events had been gradually prepared to be the recipient of a revelation prepared by the ancestral traditions and a succession of affairs which raised them from misery and slavery to liberty and triumph, and roused them from despair and stupor to the very pinnacle of enthusiasm and inspiration. Here a supernatural fact announces itself with natural antecedents, a purely intellectual fact with a whole nation as its witness. No other revelation in any sacred book of Jews, Christians, Mohammedans or Heathens steps upon the stage of existence with that force of internal evidence as did the Sinaic revelation. The reader of those chapters of Scriptures is forced to declare the whole as a piece of invention or accept it as a fact, no middle ground is possible. No sane man can *prove* it an invention, while in favor of its truth there are also the following grounds:

The second point in the historical argument is the united testimony of the whole Hebrew people during all the centuries after that revelation. The Hebrew people developed itself and its institutions, its religion and its government and its code of ethics, its character and its entire history from and upon that very foundation of the Sinaic revelation. Three thousand years of a nation's life and history are perhaps the most conclusive evidence to establish a fact, and this evidence supports the Sinaic revelation. The Hebrews never denied, never gainsaid, never doubted. The Bible is full of glorifications of Sinai, yea, the whole Bible is built upon it. The Apocrypha and the Grecian-Jewish writings know and acknowledge it. The Mishna and the Talmud, the entire ancient Jewish literature is brimful of it. The Jewish metaphysicians and philosophers down to Mendelssohn and Steinheim corroborate and expound it. The most glorious minds of the nation expounded and promulgated it. Prophet and sage, philosopher and historian, reasoner and believer accepted it; what right has any rational man to doubt it? Here is the testimony of a nation from the very beginning and all the centuries of its long history, who, from any standpoint of reason, will gainsay it? "Guard thy tongue against evil (speech) and thy lips from speaking deceit."

That is not all, however, the witnesses are still more numerous and the testimony much stronger. The two systems of Christianity and the Islam are built upon the substance of the Sinaic revelation because it is a fact, consequently all their votaries from the very beginning to this day acknowledge it, and believe it, and stand in awe before the thunders and lightnings of Sinai. The fundamental idea of right and wrong, truth and falsehood,

God, man and their relation, human duty, dignity and destiny, " What man must do to live with them," the guide, the chart, the compass for man and nations, among Jews, Christians and Mohammedans are taken from the Sinaic revelation and based upon the fact of revelation. So God declared we should do, is the fundamental principle of civilization which directs all and to which all conscientious men, consciously or unconsciously, appeal.

Therefore, while Jew and Mohammedan contradict the special Christian revelation, and Jew and Christian deny the special Mohammedan revelation, and the very nation among whom Christianity was begotten gainsay its divinity; all of them, Jew, Christian and Mohammedan, unanimously affirm, confirm and indorse the Sinaic revelation. No other revelation is supported by similar pillars of testimony, none rests upon as solid a historical evidence, none can boast upon that *argumentum a consensu gentium* as the Sinaic revelation, so that the worst of all skeptics, if he reason correctly, and the strictest adherent to the all-sufficiency of human reason could only come to the conclusion, if any revelation is true, the Sinaic revelation must be; if this is not all the others are fabrics of falsehood. But then we would have to say, all men are neither fools nor knaves, all men know more than any one, if all men believe and have believed a falsehood, then all of them reason erroneously, consequently human reason must be erroneous, which the advocates of the all-sufficiency of human reason could not admit without gross self-contradiction. The historical testimony as it is undoubtedly before us, confirms the fact of the Sinaic revelation, and this is the only species of evidence to establish a fact in the consciousness of reason.

Well, then, here is the main point of "Agreement" among Jews and Gentiles, among all religions and all special forms of civilization in the Nineteenth Century. Starting from this solid basis, in which reason and faith concur, we ought to be able to overcome our "Disagreements" in the very light and spirit of our age and our country. Let all good men reason to bring forth agreement from disagreement and replace the fanatical and fantastical war cries by salutations of peace. Silence the savage martial song and sing the beautiful melodies of fraternizing humanity, that the Psalmist's benign vision be fulfilled, "Jehovah will give might to his people, Jehovah bless his people with peace."

V.

THE LAWS OF MOSES AND THE LAW OF PROGRESS.

The progress of the human family is a law of history, hence a revelation of Providence as true and sacred as the origination of the cosmos, which revealed the power and wisdom of the Maker of all things in the beginning. Whoever counteracts the laws of nature is a sinner, whose punishment is inevitable. Whoever rebels against the law of history, and the progress of the human family is such a law, can be no less a sinner against the same Maker, Providence, the Eternal God, who says, "Mine is vengeance and recompense." By accumulation of the material progress is achieved. Hence when and where the means of preservation and promulgation were limited, the progress was slow, almost imperceptible at certain times and places. These means having grown to perfection almost by typography, the application of steam and electricity, the progress is now so much more marked, rapid and universal than heretofore. Still it is always the same law of progress which underlies the history of the race, enacted by the Creator of man and engrossed on human nature.

It is evident, therefore, that no institution, no precept or system of precepts, no form of worship and no code of ethics claiming to be of divine origin, could have the tendency of stopping or even retarding the onward march of humanity from lower to higher conditions. Therefore no religious system nor any form of government which hinders mankind in its natural progress could be of divine origin. Its course bears the imprint and historical evidence of its own transitory nature; while that which is originally divine is eternal.

If this postulate is true, and all of us feel instinctively that it must be, while no honest student of history can gainsay it, then the question arises, what about the Laws of Moses? If all of them are of direct divine origin, each and all of them must be eternal and subservient to the progress of humanity. This is evidently not the case. The Laws of Moses contain plan and specification for the construction of a sanctuary and its furniture, built but once and then never again. They advance minute prescriptions of a sacrificial polity, a Levitical priesthood, their garments, performances and observances, their required cleanness and the taxes and gifts of the people secured to them by law; all of which were not observed by the Hebrews in the Babylonian captivity, although there were among them prophets like Ezekiel, and have not been observed by them ever since the Romans under Titus destroyed the temple and altar at Jerusalem, and none of their most pious teachers admonished them to observe these laws outside of the Holy Land. On the contrary those teachers maintained that to offer a sacrifice outside of Mount Moriah was a sin punishable with *Kharath* " to be cut off." And yet none can maintain that the reinstitution of the sacrificial polity would advance the progress or any special interest of humanity.

Again the penal laws of Moses, capital punishment included, in course of time were radically changed and a number of them abolished by the ancient Hebrews themselves and in Palestine, where they lived under the Law and were devoutly attached to it. Yet no philanthropic jurist will maintain that the re-enforcement of those penal laws would advance the cause of humanity and accelerate the progress of justice, liberty and enlightenment.

The same is the case with the laws concerning the Jubilee and Sabbath years, together with the right of possession and personal freedom connected with them, as laid down by Moses, and they are fundamental in his policy; and his democratic or theocratic form of government, which was changed already in the time of Samuel and Saul; and quite a number of external observances which Jew, Christian and Mohammedan fail to observe.

Again, while the Deutero-Isaiah told his people that as rain and snow coming down from heaven return not thither before they have accomplished their object in enlivening, fructifying and blessing the earth and the offspring of her lap, " So, even so, shall be my word which goeth forth from my mouth; it shall not return empty to me, unless it hath done what I desire, and hath caused to prosper as I sent it." (Isaiah lv. 10, 11.) While the last of the prophets, Malachi, admonished his people, " Remember ye the law of Moses my servant which I commanded unto him in Horeb"; and Jesus of Nazareth is reported to have said that not a tittle nor an iota of the Law should remain unfulfilled, that he had not come to abolish but to fulfill the Law; and according to his biographers he did obey and practice the Laws of Moses and even those of the Pharisees. We find, on the other hand, that the Hebrews in the Babylonian captivity did not observe the whole law; that even Ezra and Nehemiah changed some and abolished other provisions of the Law; that the ancient expounders thereof established the rules, (1) that commendatory laws depending in practice upon a fixed time are not obligatory upon woman; and (2) that all laws depending in practice upon the locality or soil of Palestine are obligatory upon none outside thereof; and Paul of Tarsus, on the same principle, declared the Law abrogated for all his converts who resided outside of Palestine, as he was acknowledged merely as the Apostle to the Gentiles, hence those living outside of Palestine. And now there is a Babylonian confusion among Jews and Gentiles, all of them acting without a principle in regard to the laws of Moses. Now they tell us that you must do this, or you must not do that, for so God commanded through Moses; and the next moment they do as they please, as if a Moses or a Law of Moses had never existed. They speak of the divinity of the Law, or even the divinity of the Law, the Prophets and the Gospel, and eat blood and the flesh of the swine, cut short the hairs of their heads and shave their beards, wear garments of linen and woolen mixed, pray to Jesus and make Sabbath laws for Sunday, as though there were no such book in existence as the Bible. There is an utter confusion with a perfect absence of principle in this matter, and nobody can tell why or wherefore. And yet it can not be denied that the word of God must be eternal. No righteous man must live and act contrary to the revealed will of God. Revelation can not be changed by revelation. "God is no man that he should lie, nor the son of man that he should repent." Eternity is the criterion of the revealed. Nor can it be denied that there are laws in the code of Moses which the progress of humanity, the progress of ages, of necessity, did change and they could not be enforced again. And it must be admitted that one of the objects of the Sinaic revelation was that the people should believe in Moses. At the very threshold of the history of revelation Moses objected, "And they will not believe in me," and God assured him they would. At the Red Sea it is stated particularly, "And they believed in Jehovah and Moses, His servant." But this belief, produced by miracle, says Moses Maimonides, was infirm and untenable; therefore God says again to Moses, "Behold, I come to thee in the thick cloud, that the people hear when I speak unto thee, and they shall believe also in thee forever." And it appears his contemporaries did, when after the revelation on Sinai they said, "Speak thou to us and we will hearken, but let not God speak to us, lest we die;" and posterity testified, "And there did not arise a prophet in Israel like Moses, whom God instructed face to face."

Here is evidently a dilemma for the conscientious man who seeks a firm standpoint in the word of God. He feels the necessity of being an honest and upright man, a child of the living God in time and eternity. He wants certainty in all matters of rectitude and righteousness, certainty for his hopes and expectations, certainty to satisfy his conscience; and yet he dare not rebel against the law of progress, he can not change the past events of history which influenced him and society to be as they are. This inquiry is certainly of paramount importance to all good men, all who desire to be right with God and man, to all who are not foolish enough to believe that " my individual reason and conscience suffice to guide me heavward, and to form my character according to the law of God." Who shall give us a decisive answer to this query? Where is the authority upon which we could safely rely in this point? I think the best authority on this point must be Moses himself. Like every wise legislator he ought to point out to us which of his laws were intended for all generations and are universal, and which of them were temporary and local or tribal only, when and how the latter might be amended or repealed in the progress of ages. Let us see.

The Sinaic revelation with its universal precepts and categories of the moral law announces itself as THE Law of the Covenant between God and Israel, hence between God and all human beings who are of Israel in spirit and practice. This is certainly the sense of the 5th and 6th verses of Exodus xix. If you will do as I command, says God to Israel, you shall be to me a peculiar people, a select nation for the education of the human family, " For mine is the whole earth," says the divine message, which is the home of God's children all. And then again God said to Moses, to write down THESE WORDS, upon which depend the covenant between him and Israel; "And he did write upon the tables the words of the covenant, the ten words," the Decalogue. (Exodus xxxiv. 27, 28.) And again, in the last days of his life, when the hoary redeemer and father of his nation reviewed the past and admonished them to obey God's Law in the future, that they may live and prosper, and referring again to the glorious event of the Sinaic revelation and the covenant, he tells them again almost in the same words, "And he told you his covenant, what he commanded you to do, the ten words; and he wrote them upon two tables of stone." (Deut. iv. 13.) It is concerning the substance of the Sinaic revelation that all the people unanimously exclaimed, "Whatever God hath said, we will do" (Exodus xix. 8), and concerning the ordinances added by Moses they added to the above, "And we will hearken." (*Ibid.* xxiv. 7.) No pen could express an author's intention clearer, more distinct, and more precise than the pen of Moses placed before posterity the great facts, that God's covenant with Israel, hence His universal and eternal covenant with man, that covenant of the divine love which the Father makes with His children, of elevation, redemption and salvation, depends on no other law, precept, doctrine, reasoning or revelation, besides the substance of the Sinaic revelation. As perspicuously as words can express thoughts, he tells his people, as long as you will obey and do that which God has taught you in that Sinaic revelation, of which the Decalogue is the briefest abstract which could be made, so long shall you be God's people, the children of the house, the educators of mankind, the unifying element of the human race upon the eternal constitution of righteousness and under the glorious dome of Heaven's truth and the Father's love. The covenant between God and man, this is the clear sense of Scriptures, depends on God's Law and man's obedience to the best of his knowledge. The righteous man is the child of God, and God's Law defines in a few words the signification of that most important term, by which man rises to the height of perfection and eternal life, and the human family is united and fraternized to prosperity and happiness.

If this is so, the question arises, where are the glory and greatness of Moses whom God instructed face to face? Where are the greatness, usefulness and necessity of the laws of Moses? We answer, Moses would be great and glorious enough, if he was only the redeemer of Israel, the first successful apostle of liberty and human rights, and the organ of divine revelation, the first bearer and exponent of that redeeming truth which elevates man to a child of God. But he was more than that, he was the greatest legislator and statesman in history, whose legislation and political creation outlasted all centuries and all revolutions of the past. He bequeathed to posterity the most wonderful five-act drama in the five books of Moses, the most colossal and indestructible monument in the immortal Hebrew people and most lasting influence upon the legislation of the civilized world.

Critics who find ever as many mistakes and shortcomings in Moses are either too unwise or too uncharitable to judge a great statesman, whose object of existence is concentrated in the problem which he solves. The problem which Moses solved was immense. He moved a whole nation from their homes to the wilderness, removed from the necks of the multitude the shackels of slavery, organized out of that material an ideal nation to outlast all others, and did all that not only in direct opposition to the fundamental conceptions and domineering institutions of Egypt and the most advanced nations of the age, but on the eternal principles of human rights and liberty, justice, equality, pure ethics and religion, on the very precepts and laws of the Sinaic revelation. No wonder that he was obliged to tolerate many an inherited evil and subject it to the control of law, to be gradually eradicated, and was under the dire necessity of doing things which, under other circumstances, would appear unjust and contrary to his own laws. Such a statesman, the master mind of such a gigantic enterprise must not be judged like other men or legislators.

The mystery of the Mosaic legislation is in the point that he realized and embodied the precepts and laws of the Sinaic revelation in the laws, institutions and organism of a nation, under the influence of circumstances over which he had no control, to be placed in a country which had to be conquered by the force of arms, and to maintain there its independence surrounded by nations of entirely different and hostile conceptions, habits, beliefs, forms of government, religion and ethics. That was his great work, which he accomplished under the direction and with the aid of the Almighty, the governing power and reason of the universe, to whom he stood as much nearer than other men, nearer even than all the other prophets, as the man above the storm-clouds on the top of Mount Blanc stands higher and sees clearer than the man groping about in the mists of the valley.

Every law of Moses incarnates a Sinaic precept and bases upon a Sinaic law, reducing it to practice under the peculiar circumstances to be controlled by law. Precisely the same is the case with all his institutions. So he himself informs us more than once. As, for instance, speaking of the revelation and its substance, he continues, "And God commanded me at that time to teach you ordinances and statutes, that you do them in the land, to which you pass over to possess it." (Deut. iv. 14.) He only claims to have made ordinances and statutes on the underlying precepts and laws from Sinai, to be observed in that land and nowhere else. He was too meek and too wise a man to presume that his ordinances and statutes should remain unchanged, when the circumstances always change. Therefore he established an authority, a supreme council to expound, extend, amend and change laws (Deut. xvii. 8–13), and told his people to do as that supreme council may decide or ordain. The underlying principles of the Mosaic law are eternal, they are of the precepts and laws revealed on Mount Sinai; the law, any law, can be no more than the temporary incarnation of a principle, to meet, direct and control temporary circumstances and emergencies. The Mosaic law made the universal substance of the revelation practical and national, but it did not place itself in opposition to the eternal law of progress; on the contrary it acknowledges this universal law of Providence and modulates itself accordingly. We still believe in Moses and his divine authority, as far as he claims it.

Therefore it is the duty of every conscientious man to know and understand the Sinaic revelation first, then the substance and spirit of the Mosaic laws, and especially their underlying principles and precepts, to be guided by them in a life of righteousness and of preparation for life eternal. We can not do more than this. We are not expected to do better. In this point, we think, Jew and Gentile might agree, and reason confirms it. But here quite a number of questions arise in regard to the practice and the proper authority to expound the law, which, our time being over, we can not discuss this evening, but I promise to take them up one after the other in the next following lectures. As a general rule let us understand that revelation, like creation, like the work of genius, bursts into existence suddenly and completely.

Evolution can only succeed it, development and practical application can only follow it. "Once God hath spoken (although), twice have I heard it." "It was a great voice, and it continued not," it was never repeated. Since then reason and conscience are the two Cherubim above the ark, from between which we hear the benign voice of the Eternal God.

VI.

THE HIGHEST AUTHORITY AFTER REVELATION.

Although it must be admitted that this age of emancipation combats against authority, yet it can not be denied that we are always guided and governed by it; the authority of persons, books, institutions, inherited or acquired habits and passions, which we consider superior to ourselves or we consider ourselves inferior to them. The child is led by the authority of parents, nurses, tutors and older companions. The school-boy believes in his text-books, and many remain school-boys all their life-time. With all our pride and self-esteem we accept the best part of our knowledge upon the authority of others. As a general thing we believe and know that which others have imposed upon us, and like best to do that to which others force us most gently, by authority after all.

There are certain forms of authority which can never be overcome successfully. For instance, the authority of reason imperiously demands submission. Whatever human reason appreciates as true and good, useful and advantageous, will at last be modulated as law or laws and govern you, me and all, whatever time it may take the logical element to overcome and overthrow its illogical antagonist.

So we will never be able to overcome the authority of society over the individual. Any one must submit to many, as many know better than one, and none can step out entirely of the magic circle of society. That supposition that one may be right and all the world about him wrong, is a hypothesis similar to the missing link in Darwinism, which never had existence in reality. Man at best is a clear focus, in which the latent thoughts of his time converge and are reflected in acceptable words and deeds. It is only an inch or two that any man, with the exception of rare genius, overtowers the society in which he lives. Lower your sails, top-lofty demi-gods. Again, the method has not yet been discovered to throw off the authority of our own making. We consider it the mildest form, which it is not always, and submit to it with good grace. Here, then, are three different forms of authority, from which man can not emancipate himself, hence he must regulate them and shape himself to suit these three despots.

The authority of our own making, made concrete among us by a host of executive, legislative and judiciary officers, elected or appointed directly or indirectly, as the case may be, represents the authority of society and is identical with it; hence in the main the two authorities could be counted as one only.

The questions, how this authority must be managed to be least oppressive to the individual or to minorities, and how much of his natural right the individual must relinquish to that authority, are as old as society, and have been practically solved by the various forms of government and the huge library of laws which are the bane of the law-student's existence. The debates over these questions form the substance of history, and were the primary causes of oppression and despotism now, of revolts and revolutions then, of periods of satisfaction and much longer intervals of dissatisfaction, until at the eleventh hour of the eighteenth century we have come to the conclusion, that the questions must be solved on three principles, viz, the representative form of government, decentralization of power, and the appointment of rulers by those who are to be ruled by them. It is the mildest form of coercion, forcing the individual most gently to submit to the authority of society, and is, therefore, most acceptable to him.

If this is the most proper form of government—and the most advanced nations, together with the most enlightened and philanthropic individuals of all other nations, avow that it is—then in this one important point Scripture is being fulfilled, when God said to Moses, "And also in thee they shall believe forever." It was Moses, the man Moses, who first proclaimed liberty and equality as the divine right of man, and God's justice as the only crown and scepter of nations, "For justice is God's." It was that same man Moses who, for the first time in history, laid down those three principles of human government, and reared upon them the structure of the Hebrew State, to become in proper time the ideal and model of nations. Please take up once more your Bible, read that old, old *Thorah* again, and you will, perhaps, be astonished to find in it those very principles which, after centuries of disobedience, misery, bloodshed and heaven-defying wrongs, we have been forced to acknowledge as the salvation of man on earth. Right at the threshold Moses informs us that God, making His covenant with Abraham, promised him the land of Canaan, the government of God, and the nation composed of nations, to descend from him. Thou shalt be *Ab Hamon Goyim*, "the father of a multitude of nations," which is explained afterward by *Kehal Goyim*, "a congregation of nations" (Gen. xvii. 4; xxviii. 3; xlviii. 4), was God's promise to Abraham, which can only signify a nation composed of nations, an *E pluribus unum*. On this principle of decentralization the blessing or last will of Jacob (Genesis xlix.) establishes the twelve tribes organization, which was faithfully maintained in Goshen. On this fundamental fact of twelve independent tribes united in one sovereignty Moses constructed the Hebrew State; and so the universal republic will be constructed, when the long and bloody war in the human family shall be ended, and peace established and secured.

Then again Moses informs us (Numbers xi. 11 to 25) that God told him to organize the Council of Seventy Elders, to introduce the representative form of government also in the whole nation, as it did exist among the individual tribes; and he did so, and made it permanent (Deut. xvii. 8 to 13), and reared his system of government on it, so that, with the exception of times of rebellion by the people or its kings, there always existed a supreme representative body in Israel under different names, as the Council of Elders, the Great Synod, the Law Court of the High-priests, the Law Court of the Asmoneans, the Sanhedrin, the Great Assembly called *Va'ad hag-Gadol* and such other names; so that the rabbis of the Talmud came to the conclusion that the commandment to have a Sanhedrin is always obligatory on Israel in Palestine and outside thereof. (See *Sanhedrin* in *Yad ha-Chasakah.*)

And again that man Moses commanded his people (Deut. xvi. 18), " Judges and bailiffs shalt thou give unto thee in all thy gates which the Lord thy God will give thee, for thy tribes, and they shall judge the people a righteous judgment." Also the tribal judges and executive officers, we are thus informed, were to be elected or appointed by the people, " *Thou shalt give unto thee,*" and by no other power or authority. Only in time of war, in the organization of the army of defense, Moses permits an exception to this rule, and allows the elected bailiffs to appoint the officers of the host. (Deut. xx. 9.)

So the lawgiver in the wilderness has laid down the three leading principles to secure and modify the authority of society, and to render it least oppressive to the individual; and so we, at this end of the nineteenth century, feel ourselves obliged to acknowledge his superior wisdom. Let us see now how he dealt with the authority of reason.

Reason is one of those cases which can not be reached by a statute of limitation. It has no boundaries. It can not be limited. Man will reason in spite of all danger and peril, even in the face of death. He reflects on the unknowable, and ponders over perpetual motion and the quadrature of the circle. The ocean is not too deep and heaven not too high for reason's strides toward omnipresence, time and space limit not its attempt at infinity. The only misfortune is, that every man reasons with an individualized intellect and under the influence of accidents. Therefore the diversity of judgments, conclusions, views and opinions. And yet everybody is governed by his own reason, which produces anarchy and oppression by the authority of reason. This diversity of opinions and judgments proves that reason is not infallible, as that anarchy and oppression furnish the evidence that unaided human reason is insufficient to govern society and satisfy the individuals thereof. If reason is to govern, the question arises, whose reason? Answer this question as you please, say one potentate or many heads united should govern, you always exclude the great multitude, each of whom has a reason and a judgment of his own, tyrannized over by that one potentate or those many heads.

The expediency to which nations and communities had recourse was the constitution, the charter, or a bill of rights, supposed to be the product of a nation's reason, to prescribe limits to the power of rulers, legislators and judges. It is better than nothing, and answers the purpose temporarily, as is evident in the history of nations from the frequent and radical changes of those constitutions and charters, none of which has answered the purpose permanently, for each of which is after all the product of some individual intellects, which can not comprehend the judgment of all and under all circumstances; and none could be universal.

How did Moses settle this difficult point? Or rather how does he satisfy us on this point? "And the man Moses was very meek," Scripture reports of him. He understood what it meant when God told him, "No man can see me and live"; he knew and comprehended well what so many of us are so slow to admit, viz: that human reason has its limits, the individual intellect has its boundaries, beyond which it can not go; it must stop somewhere, and so it must start from certain fixed and positive points, where all questions of why and wherefore became illegitimate. Reason itself must stop before its own authority. Ask why this azure dome above your head appears to your eyes blue and spherical, why should it not be rose colored and of oval form? Ask wherefore the stars are clustered in heaven in such irregular groups, and the distances between them are so different? Ask why and wherefore is the lily white and the tulip red, or why and wherefore has man no wings, not four legs or four hands like other animals? Or, if you please, ask what is substance, spirit, matter, force, sensitiveness or consciousness, and you will be convinced that you have arrived at the boundaries of reason, for the wisest of the wise, the princes of science and philosophy can not answer those questions. We know not, is the humiliating confession of the individual intellect and the aggregated wisdom of mankind. We start from a number of given facts and reason from analogy, by comparison and interpretation. We must stop somewhere, because we can not start out with zero, and wherever we stop to start from, we must have facts of nature or history, or the authority of a superhuman reason.

So, exactly so did Moses settle this difficult point for his people and for all nations and generations. There is a supreme reason and goodness, superhuman and supermundane, and that is the eternal Jehovah, and he makes known to you the universal facts, before which the individual intellect must stop and from which it must start. These moral facts have been actualized in the doings and teachings of the fathers, and are made known to you now under the thunders and lightnings of Sinai as the law of the covenant, the fundamental law of the nation and the nations of all generations and localities. So Moses said to his people, and so he speaks to the world forever. From those facts thus given, he added, God commanded me to start out, develop and establish a national code of religion, government and ethics; and starting out with those divine facts, and the unalloyed intention only to actualize those divine teachings in laws and institutions, to realize truth and righteousness, prosperity and happiness to you and all nations who will do like you, I know that God speaks to me and through me, I know that God is with me, instructs and directs me, has chosen you and me to carry out this sublime scheme of salvation. So Moses protected himself and his system, his people and his fellow-men against the despotism and anarchy of individual reason, the ignorance and short-sightedness of the human intellect. Whatever any prophet might tell you, he said to his people, you shall listen to him except when he says, " Let us go and let us worship other gods," then that prophet shall be put to death. This, however, is the beginning of rebellion against the substance of the Sianic revelation, against which none is permitted to go. You dare not go behind the axioms in any science. You must not go against the facts of nature and history. Here are the axioms and facts of God's law, here you must stop, from this point you must start.

The highest authority therefore after revelation is the Law of Moses, not indeed always in its letter, but always in its spirit, as every law and institution thereof rests upon a Sinaic principle, which does not pass away as times and circumstances and with them the letters of a law and the utility of an institution do. Not only is the promise made to Moses, announced in the same revelation, " And they shall also believe in thee forever," to be fulfilled; but we have the positive conviction, at which we have arrived at this end of the ninteenth century, that in the main principles of public government Moses was as correct as in his theology; that his sanitary laws, his marital laws, his martial laws, his emancipation laws, his charity laws, and above all his broad and humane injunctions, " Love thy neighbor as thyself" and " Ye shall love the stranger," are as sublime and divine as was his lofty conception of Deity and humanity, because all was of one cast, all one and the same realization of the same Sinaic principle, although shaped here and there to correspond with the habits and circumstances of that time, people and country. Take for instance his charity laws, and remember that he secured to the poor, widow, orphan and stranger the gleanings of the field, vineyard and olive orchard, the sheaf forgotten in the field, the corner of the standing corn not to be cut by the owner, and such other gifts. You will see instantly that this particular giving of alms does not relate to the millionaires and merchant princes of these or other days, and can find no literal application among the husbandmen of all ages. The letter of the law is abrogated, but its inherent spirit, its underlying principle is eternal. It is as obligatory to-day as it was when Moses announced it in the name of God. This is the case with every law and institution of Moses, which is tribal, local or otherwise accommodating in its wording. Therefore the Law of Moses is the highest authority after revelation.

For Israel, you want me to add? For Israel only? In the face of truth, I can not and dare not make such an assertion. Revelation can not be undone by revelation. Whatever the Father of mankind has given to his children, belongs to all of them. The words of many Mosaic laws and the nature of his institutions must of necessity be tribal, local and transitory; the underlying principles are eternal and universal, they are the common property of all men, they are obligatory upon all nations and generations. This is the authority given to reason, given to communities and nations, according to the very words of Moses, to start from the axioms of the Sinaic revelation; to incarnate those principles, as Moses did and commanded his successors to do, in constitutions and institutions, in laws and ordinances, in religious, political and social practice. No individual reasoner, and no nation has a right to deviate from this course, prescribed for all of them by the Almighty God. The progress of mankind to prosperity and happiness, to solidarity, humanity and piety depends upon this very principle; and most all miseries of the human family rose from the violation thereof. You have not done, and you do not do as God has commanded you from Sinai, therefore idolatry and slavery, fanaticism and oppression, immorality and ignorance make you miserable; such is the voice of God to the nations. Obey and live, hearken and be blessed. Proclaim freedom and equality to all, justice and righteousness for all, charity and good will among all, slay not, steal not, debauch not, lie not and covet not, honor your parents, worship God and keep the Sabbath holy, be conscientious with the laws of God, and impart them to your children, let all this be impressed upon your constitutions and institutions, and you will be the children of the living God. This is the import of the Sinaic revelation, the message of the Almighty to all nations. If you are anxious to do right and to live, to prosper and progress to happiness, know, understand and comprehend well the Sinaic revelation, and be guided by God's teachings. If you are anxious to apply those divine doctrines to the government of nations, learn in and from the Law of Moses how principles are to be incarnated in practical laws and institutions with reference to time, locality and historical antecedents. God is eternal, his word is eternal, and in this His word He promised to Moses, " And also in thee they shall believe forever."

VII.

SINAI AND CALVARY COMPARED FROM THE ETHICAL STANDPOINT.

That which is right to one ought to be right to all; and that which is wrong for one must be wrong for all—is the cardinal principle of divine ethics in contra-position to such human forms of government, in which might is the source of right (which is also a weak point of Baruch Spinoza), the privileges of some persons and classes and the oppression of others form the substratum of law, as in the feudal system of government, so that the main object of law and government is, to invent and apply the means for one class to check, subject and control the other class. The form of government basing strictly and exclusively upon the moral law is ethical, while all forms of government basing right upon might and law upon existing wrongs, are martial, a state of warfare with the enforced intervals of armistice between, among the classes and persons of the same commonwealth, and consequently also of one commonwealth against the other. This martial form of government prevailed among all nations of antiquity, and reached its culminating point in the Roman Empire. The ethical form of government originated in the Sinaic revelation and the Law of Moses, and always remained the ideal of the Hebrew State, however frequent the rebellions of kings, priests and people may have been. All laws of antiquity, from Fo, Thoth or Hermes, down to the Justinian code, including all philosophies of corresponding ages and nations, are based upon the martial form of government; while the whole body of Jewish Law in Bible, Talmud and post-Talmudical casuists bases upon the ethical form of government. Mistakes were made, of course, by this and that ruler, sage or teacher, but the ground form is invariably as stated.

The ethical form of government originating in the Sinaic revelation, we may call it divine, as the martial form of government may be called human, although it is, and was often far from being humane. To this may be added, if Judaism signifies the body of doctrine contained in the Sinaic revelation, then the ethical form of government is one of the principal elements thereof, and is in so far Jewish as it was revealed and commanded first to the Hebrew people, which was appointed to be *Am Kadosh*, " Holy Nation," in its policy, as well as in its polity, in its government as well as in its religion, in its administration of human affairs, as well as in its divine worship and the formation of private character, all of which to center in and radiate from the one fundamental doctrine of the One Holy God who delights in purity, justice and human happiness, and destined man to find his prosperity and happiness in his endeavor to do justice, to love purity and benignity, and to walk in uprightness before God.

Modern history begins, as is generally maintained, with the origin of Christianity. The Christianity of history, as history developed it, points to Mount Calvary for its starting point, as Judaism points to Mount Sinai. It looks upon the mundane existence, passion, death and resurrection of Jesus of Nazareth as a second revelation, not indeed superseding the Sinaic revelation, for revelation can not undo revelation, but supplementing and explaining it for the benefit also of the Gentiles.

It is not my intention at present to dispute or discuss the alleged fact; for the sake of argument I admit the standpoints of both Judaism and Christianity, and will merely attempt to solve the problem whence the moral law has its authority, from Sinai or Calvary. Permit me to remark right here that every religion is beneficial to man, because every one, the rudest feticism not excepted, contains rational and ethical elements, or else man could not have believed in it. Such is the nature of man, that fiction and falsehood prove acceptable to him only in connection with truth and righteousness. With every religious idea which rises in the mind of man, he rises above the brutal sphere to the region of ideality, and as he rises thus he becomes a better man, less governed by the lower passions and animal instincts, and more eager for a higher and nobler life. Every religious idea is an act of emancipation to the individual, liberating him from the despotism of sensuality and elevating him to the freedom of mind and spirit, in the same ratio as that religious idea contains truth and the incentive for righteousness. No reasoner, unless he be a fanatic, will oppose religion in any form. It is man's *sanctum sanctorum*, which none must enter except the high-priest of human reason, and then only on the Day of Atonement with the overruling idea of peace and atonement, justice and good will to all.

Let me add here that Christianity has done so large an amount of good and is doing it now, that it certainly must command respect as the religion of three hundred and more millions of people. Least among all men the religious Jew dare attack Christianity with any weapons except the most rational and most charitable, as he maintains that whatever is true and benevolent in Christianity is taken from Judaism, so that the Gospels also are compilations of more ancient Jewish sentences and sentiments, an allegation which but lately Professor August Wuensche proved to be a fact, as was done before him by Kalisch, Wise, Nork, Lightfoot and others. The Christianity or rather Christology of history, built up by priests, councils, potentates, legislators and dogmatic reasoners, which has only its most distant roots in Calvary, like the Talmuds of the Jews in the Law, and the traditions of the Mohammedans in the Koran, has never been finally established in any particular point with the consent and to the satisfaction of all Christians. Like everything of historical growth, it must be human and subject to the law of dissolution, hence also to free discussion and commentation, without any attack on religion itself. Christology is not Christianity, and dogmatism is not religion. Jesus of Nazareth advanced no dogmas. Hence, from the Christian standpoint it must be admitted that whatever has not been said by Jesus, can not be placed in juxtaposition with the substance of the Sinaic revelation.

Coming back to the ethical standpoint the question arises, as far as the government, laws and institutions of nations are concerned, did Jesus add anything to the Sinaic revelation or abrogate any of its provisions and doctrines? You may look upon it from any known standpoint, and you will always feel obliged to answer this question in the negative. He did not add thereto, nor did he diminish therefrom. He could not. Nobody believing in revelation can, as little as one can improve the totality of creation. He told that young man who inquired of him what he must do to be saved, the very words of the Decalogue, and maintained even in regard to the Laws of Moses, that not a tittle or an iota thereof should remain unfulfilled, that he had not come to abolish but to fulfill the Law. He did not say that the Sabbath day was abolished, abrogated or changed. When the Pharisees censured his disciples for plucking ears in the field on the Sabbath day; he merely said, as is also in the Jewish writings (*Mechilta*), that man was not made for the Sabbath, but the Sabbath was made for man. If it had been his intention to propose any change in the Sinaic revelation, he must have said so then and there, instead of debating the question from the Pharisean standpoint.

Again, according to the Gospels and Epistles, the main object of Jesus was to establish the Kingdom of Heaven. If you define this Kingdom from the Jewish standpoint, it is a translation of the Hebrew *Malchuth Shamayim* or the Grecian "theocracy," and it was the aim and object of Jesus to restore in Israel the ancient democratic theocracy, as a few decades before him the representatives of a great party in Israel had asked it of Pompey, and as during the life-time of Jesus other representatives of the same party asked it of Agustus. In this case, of course, there could be no idea that Jesus wanted to change an iota in the Sianic revelation, which is the very groundwork and rock of the theocracy. Look upon it from the Christian standpoint and you must admit that the Kingdom of Heaven means nothing in this life and this sublunar world; it begins with death and refers exclusively to the salvation of the soul in the life hereafter. Therefore he is reported to have said, " My Kingdom is not of this world." This is repeated in substance by both Peter and Paul in their respective Epistles, who admonished the primitive Christians to submit to any and every political government, to obey him who bears the sword of authority, as God must have given it to him, and their Christ had not come to interfere with the temporal affairs of man this side of the boundary line of death. Therefore Paul taught that faith, hope and love were sufficient to guide the redeemed ones to salvation in life eternal. Hence it must be admitted, if Jesus had nothing to do with the affairs of this world, nothing with the government of nations and the rights of man, he had nothing to do with ethics, which concerns man in this state of existence first and foremost, and could at no time have thought of adding to or taking away from the Sinaic revelation.

The Sermon on the Mount, whether it was actually delivered by Jesus as it is recorded by Matthew, or whether only a portion thereof was delivered at some other place, as Luke maintains (chapter vi. verse 21), or whether it was not delivered at all, as both Mark and John appear to admit by their silence regarding that important document, or whether it was compiled by Matthew of sentences, which the Church held to have been uttered by Jesus; that very Sermon on the Mount, concerning which Dr. Zipser, Prof. Wuensche and others have furnished the evidence, that every sentiment thereof has its parallel in the old Bible and Talmud; that very Sermon on the Mount adds not an iota to and takes none away from the ethics contained in the Sinaic revelation, or even in the Laws of Moses. The eccentricities and amplifications supposed to be contained in it are easily explained by the circumstances and affairs of that very age. The very patriotic Jews of that day certainly hated their Roman enemies, who oppressed and maltreated them, and were always eager to wage war upon them, which Jesus, like other disciples of the Hillel school, discouraged, maintaining that they could conquer and convert them by love, and by love only. This is the sense of " Love your enemies," although in the Christian theological sense it is after all a mere commentary to the words of Moses, " Thou shalt not hate thy brother in thy heart," " Love thy neighbor as thyself." The Roman law-courts were so corrupt, unjust and oppressive in Judea, that Jesus warned his people to have nothing to do with them; rather give a man your cloak, if he takes your undergarment; walk with him a mile, if he forces you to go one furlong; if he strikes you on one cheek, humbly offer him the other to kiss or to strike, and keep out of court. This appears to be the sense of those respective passages. But also in the Christian theological sense they are an imitation of what Jeremiah had said centuries before Jesus under similar circumstances. (Lamentations iii. 26-30.) Jesus considered him an adulterer who looked upon his neighbor's wife with impure thoughts, and Moses said, " Thou shalt not covet thy neighbor's wife." That Jesus, who went to Jerusalem to celebrate the feasts as commanded by Moses, taught the resurrection of the body exactly as the Pharisees did, risked his life in order to eat the Paschal lamb within the walls of Jerusalem and in a house exactly as the Pharisees prescribed, had certainly no idea of adding to or taking away from the substance of the Sinaic revelation or even the laws of Moses.

If Jesus has left the ethics of the Old Testament unchanged and unaltered, without addition or diminution, then Calvary has added nothing to the ethics of Sinai. Therefore, what some gentlemen are pleased to call Christian morals or Christian ethics are actually Jewish morals or Jewish ethics, which Christendom accepts and indorses. After all, perhaps, the name does not make much difference, although it is always proper to call things by their right names. It offers the advantage in this particular respect that all of us become aware how numerous, essential and important our " agreements " are, while our " disagreements" appear to be chiefly in names. In this case it appears it is also of some importance to know that all Christendom accepts and indorses in theory the ethics, the moral principles of the Sinaic revelation. The same was done by Mohammed, who accused the Jews of having eradicated all passages from their *Thorah* which prophetically referred to him and his work. It is important in this connection to know that all civilized nations agree with Moses in the principle that every State and every government of any country should be built up and conducted on the moral principle, on the accepted code of ethics, and only in case of emergencies, over which a nation has no control, is a temporary deviation from this principle admissible. Change the terms, and before you stands in bold relief the following proposition : All civilized nations agree with Moses in principle or, at least, in theory, that every State and every government of any country should be built up and conducted on the moral principle as revealed from Sinai and reduced to practice by Moses in his construction of the Hebrew State; hence all existing ethics is Sinaic. That which some gentlemen are pleased to call a Christian country, a Christian State or a Christian government, is in principle Jewish-Sinaic, purely Jewish, and only so much thereof can possibly be Christian, as that State, government or country fails to realize and carry into practice of the ethical principles of the Sinaic revelation, since Calvary has not amended the ethics of Sinai; and in so far exactly the nations are wrong and the cause of misery and self-destruction.

In order to judge these matters correctly, it must always be borne in mind that the Arabs and then the Turks stood outside of the Greco-Roman civilization by location, language and government. The elements of human government with which they entered the list of civilized nations, were fragments of Oriental despotism, remains of the Parthian-Persian system and the tribal dominion of patriarchal lawlessness. That heritage impressed itself on the Koran, the national ethics, the government, the history and fatalism of the Islamitic nations, and destroyed to a great extent the beneficial influence of the Sinaic ethics adopted by Mohammed and his expounders. Therefore, the Mohammedans are so far behind European Christians in civilization and culture. The Oriental Christians are not superior to their Islamitic neighbors in this respect. The Occidental Christians, by language, location and government, were the direct heirs of the Greco-Roman civilization and culture. However often they were overrun by barbarous hordes, revolutionized and overthrown, the ground form of that heritage always rose again from the ruins, and especially among the Latin races. Therefore, the elements of the ancient civilization afforded advantages to the Occidental nations which the Oriental nations did not possess. This is, perhaps, the main cause of the superiority of the Occidental Christians over the Oriental nations. With the Greco-Roman civilization, however, Occidental Christendom inherited also the human elements of Roman government and ethics and the feudal system of its own making. This heritage has impressed itself upon most all institutions and organizations of Christendom, exercised its nugatory influence upon the development of Christology and government, and to a great extent counteracted and neutralized the beneficial influence of the ethics from the Sinaic revelation. This is the ground-work of the historic struggle among European nations, which became most conspicuous in the struggle of the Common Law against the Civil Law, the Reformation against the established Church, the bloody revolutions which are still at work, and the attempts of science and philosophy to rise above all established authority.

The Sinaic revelation demands freedom and equality for all members of any commonwealth, and the Christian potentates built up huge despotisms, with privileged and pariah classes. Therefore, justice was made a mere hand-maid of the thrones and a body-guard of the privileged classes, to the oppression and detriment of the multitudes. Where there is no freedom and equality there can be no justice. As long as there are privileged and pariah classes, as long as men are forced into the military straight jacket against their will, as long as society anywhere is divided into lords and human dogs, there can be no freedom, no equality, no justice, hence no government of divine ethics. God said, " Thou shalt have no other gods before me," and in Christendom there are worshiped as many gods as there are supposed persons in the Deity; there were made as many demi-gods as there were emperors, kings, princes, popes, cardinals, bishops and other imitations of the Roman Pantheon. God commanded, " Remember the Sabbath-day to keep it holy," and Christendom has abolished the Sabbath-day and forces men by laws and social circumstances to sanction the violation of God's law. " Thou shalt not kill" is the divine law; war, incessant war, is the human law, and murder is frequently sanctioned besides by insufficient laws or the lack of their enforcement. " Thou shalt not steal " is another divine law, and potentates steal countries and nations, because, as they say, they need them. Government officers steal and teach the people that stealing is not so bad a business after all. And so we might go on for hours, but it would prove no more than these facts do, viz, that the misery and self-destruction of nations rise from their neglect of Sinai, their neglect to form and execute the laws on the ethics of the Sinaic revelation, to establish and maintain government on the ethical principle, as Moses constructed the Hebrew State; God promised to the seed of Abraham, "And I will be their *Elohim*," *i. e.*, absolute justice and supreme wisdom shall be the base and superstructure of their government and laws. All revolutions signify the rise of the human family toward the ethical standpoint of the Sinaic revelation. The world Judaizes and has Judaized for the last two thousand years; because there is only one standard of ethics, and that is the Revelation on Mount Sinai.

VIII.

FREEDOM THE POSTULATE OF ETHICS.

Freedom is the word which finds a joyous re-echo in every human heart. It is the Shibboleth of nations, the magic sound from the angel's trumpet of resurrection, a ray of heaven's light penetrating into the vale of darkness. For what are slavery, darkness and death but the loss of freedom, as life, light and liberty are but freedom actualized. Every living creature, like the merry lark, rising skyward with joyous song, feels that freedom is its birthright, and deprived of it, it mourns its loss and pines away even unto death. Wherever there is life there is will, and wherever there is will there is voluntary volition, which is the exercise of freedom; hence there is no life without freedom and no freedom without life. Nature is a piece of exact mechanism, hence without freedom, to the atomist and monist, who sees in it but iron and relentless laws. The theist, however, who observes in every movement and quality of matter the manifestation of the spirit and the demonstration of life, will and reason, discovers freedom in the concentric as well as in eccentric movements of nature's offspring. Not one leaflet is like the other on the same rose, no two beings are identical, no two leaves on the same tree, no two berries on the same cluster. Crystals also show individuality.

Freedom is the power (not an abstraction), inherent in the individual to rest or to move and act in obedience only to its own inherent law and its own volition. without compulsion or coercion from abroad. Being a power, it is a function which must emanate from some substance, and this can be spirit only. Hence, wherever we find freedom there must be spirit, in the individual or the cosmos. It is God in the universe, it is human mind in man, as Elihu said to Job, "Verily, it is the spirit in man, and the breath of the Almighty which giveth him understanding."

Therefore it must be legitimate to maintain that legislation against freedom is legislation against nature and nature's God. All just legislation must start with the principle of freedom, universal and individual, and must have the ultimate object in view to harmonize the volitions of many free individuals associated for their mutual benefit and the benefit of the human family. Every other legislation is unjust and contrary to the will of God manifested in His works, although it may be momentarily justfiable by emergencies, over which the legislator has no control. Permanent laws must be just and capable of universal application.

When we speak of revelation and revealed laws, we speak of freedom and justice. For the laws expressed in God's words must be in kind the same as those revealed in His works. The revealed material, as it is before us, appears to be the mundane expression of those supermundane principles of freedom and justice. God is free and just. This appears to be the starting point of the revelation. "I, *Jehovah*, am thy *Elohim*, who brought thee out of the land of Egypt, out of the house of bondage." This is premised with the words, "For mine is the whole earth"; hence God is not only mightier than the mightiest, as there exists nothing to restrain His power, the earth is His earth, the heaven is His heaven, the world is His world, all subject to His will, but He is also absolutely free, without any compulsion or coercion from abroad, and absolutely just, which is demonstrated in Israel's liberation, and understood *per se*, inasmuch as he who is absolutely potent and free could only be absolutely just.

However, God's freedom and justice are indicated there chiefly as a declaration of man's freedom, and the foundation for the divine command to man to be just and righteous. If there were no freedom and justice in God, they could not be expected in man. Whatever is not in the whole can not be expected in any part thereof. Demonstrate away freedom, by any method, from nature and nature's God, and it has no hold in human nature. Demonstrate away freedom and there is no justice, no righteousness and no virtue. The pantheists, fatalists and predestinarians know not what they do in their negation of freedom; they know not that they destroy the postulate of ethics.

Man's freedom is indicated in the very act of divine legislation, as laws could be ordained only for free agents. None will command the stone to preserve its inertia, when it can not move of its own accord. Nor will an intelligent being command the marble to become a statue, when it can only submit to the sculptor's hands. It is further indicated in the promise of reward to him who shall obey, and punishment to the disobedient, as the principle is already laid down in the premises, "And now if ye will diligently hearken unto my voice, and ye will guard my covenant, ye shall be unto me a peculiar nation," etc. Here is evidently freedom, for the possibility of obedience or disobedience is surmised. The same idea is also expressed in the obligation of the people, the promise to obey, and in the word of God addressed to Moses (Exodus xxiv. 12), "Come up to me, up the mountain, and be there, and I will give the tables of stone and the *Thorah* and the commandment which I have written to teach them"; to teach and not to impose on them as an iron necessity, the Thorah and the commandment. This presupposes freedom. Clearest, however, this principle is expressed in the event succeeding the Sinaic revelation (Exodus xx. 17), which is expounded in Deuteronomy v. 20–26, thus: The Israelites, after having heard and seen the Sinaic revelation, were very much terrified, and dreaded to hear the voice of God any longer and any more; "lest we might die," said they, and they asked Moses to bring them the laws of God, so that they need again not hear the Almighty speak. It is reported then that God consented to the people's proposition, and also said to Moses, "I wish that they had this heart (will) to fear me and to observe all my commandments all the days, that it might be well with them and their children forever." God accords the people's proposition, this sanctions the authority of human reason. God wishes they might always obey His laws, this expresses most forcibly the moral freedom of man, his accountablity to his Maker, and the principle of justice in God's government. Again and again this principle is expressed in Scriptures most clearly and forcibly (Deut. vii. 11, 12; xi. 26–28; xxx. 15, 16), so that the prophet Isaiah could announce to his people this divine oracle (i. 19), "If ye shall will and hearken, ye shall eat the good of the land; if ye shall refuse and rebel, the sword shall consume you, for so the mouth of God hath spoken." This last phrase refers to the Sinaic revelation. The two additional and apparently superflous verbs of *Thobeh*, "If you shall will," and *thema'enu*, "If you shall refuse," emphasize the doings and omissions as free will acts, in order to merit the recompense, which the prophet announces. This is the case throughout the old Bible. Freedom is the postulate of ethics and the cause of man's accountability to his Maker. Man is capable of not only receiving and understanding God's law, the expression of His will, but has also the power inherent in his spiritual nature to obey and execute it, to live and act under it, and, therefore, he is accountable to God for all his doings and omissions. There is a moral government in the world, because God is just and man is free. This, according to the Sinaic revelation, is the postulate of ethics.

Long after the close of the canon, when speculative minds analyzed those doctrines and attempted to solve the problem by discursive reasoning, the questions arose as to how much Satan has to do with the cause of human disobedience and wickedness, and again as to how much God's special grace has to do with man's power to turn from his evil ways and choose again the path of righteousness. In principle this was a limitation of man's freedom. It is not altogether he who sins, as Satan has his share in the disobedience, and we are unable to say how much of it really belongs to his Satanic majesty, and how much to the will of man. Nor is it altogether man who does that which is good and right, as God's special grace has its share in man's power for good, and none knows which share is largest God's or man's. The rabbis of the Talmud reduced the evil influence upon man to his temperament and natural disposition, and called Satan in this capacity *Yetzer ha-Rah*, to which they added that in one respect he is Satan, in another the evil disposition, and again in another the angel of death. Paul gave expression to this rabbinical doctrine in a peculiar figure of speech, saying that he had a thorn in his flesh. On the whole those rabbis paid no particular respect to Satan, and would scarcely grant him personal existence, although the later Persian rabbis had their demonology with a number of Satan stories. The Satan story in Matthew iv., partly also in Luke iv., of which Mark had no knowledge and which John did not accept, is undoubtedly an anachronism, and appears to have grown out of one verse in Mark (i. 12), which a later writer amplified in the style of the Maccabean story of Hannah and her seven sons, as in Luke, and a still later writer made of it the story as in Matthew.

As far as the special grace of God, which must move or support man, in order to enable him to overcome sin and to be righteous is concerned, the rabbis of the Talmud admit its mere existence from on high and maintain *Hab-ba letaher mesayin lo min hash-Shamayim*, " He who cometh to purify himself is assisted from Heaven," which is to say, that the divine influence supports him who, by his own free volition and resolution, endeavors to come out of the bondage of sin, without setting at naught or limiting the free will of man. It is merely maintained that the good has the assistance of Heaven. This, it appears, was also the doctrine of the primitive Christians according to Clemens, of Alexandria (*Strom.* vii. 2, 7), Origines (*De Princip.* iii. 22) and others. When the dispute between Pelagius and St. Augustine waxed hot, the doctrine was analyzed and all its elements were discussed. Pelagius adhered to the Jewish doctrine and said (*Pelag. in August. de grat. Christi* 7), somewhat to this effect; if God, by any special act of grace, must produce in us obedience to this law, then we are led into the absurdity that God gave His laws not to us but to His own grace; but they were given to our free will, which must have the power to observe them, and God's special grace may support it. But the Church had already adopted the doctrine of vicarious atonement by the passions and blood of the Redeemer. If man, by his own free volition, could overcome sin and walk in the path of righteousness, then this grace of God is inherent in all men and must be an inborn power of human nature. If so, why did Jesus suffer and die? What was gained by his passions and blood?—what has the Church to offer to her converts which they do not already possess?—where is the superiority of the Christian faith? Therefore, Augustine prevailed over Pelagius, and imposed upon the Church the whole burden of the original sin, the fall of the first parents, the sinful nature of all their descendants, the necessity of redemption in consequence thereof by faith in the redeeming power of Christ's blood, shed for the sins of his believers in all generations, and all the logical sequences of that doctrine of redemption, predestination and the damnation not only of all unbelievers, but of many believers as well, who, by the arbitrary and unjust will of God, are destined to eternal suffering.

Thomas de Aquino, the philosophical genius of the Church in the Middle Ages, was the man who formulated and established the Augustinean creed, if it may be called so. On the other hand Duns Scotus and his followers modified it by semi-Pelagian objections, and the questions were not finally settled, when the Reformation overtook the scholastic discussions. Both Melanchton and Martin Luther accepted the whole apparatus of redemption as it was formulated by Augustine and Thomas de Aquino, until Erasmus forced them to abandon that position in part, while Calvin accepted and advocated the whole theory with all its consequences. Still both Luther and Calvin agreed that man is naturally corrupt, depraved, and impotent to overcome sin and to walk in the path of righteousness. He must be redeemed by his faith in the vicarious atonement of the Redeemer if this faith comes in connection with the election of the candidate by the arbitrary will of God, according to Calvin. Both agree that man has no free will; the good can not be accomplished without the aid of the Church; human reason is under the control of Satan; and yet man is accountable to God for his deeds, and is condemned in his wickedness, although he has no free will, or, according to Qalvin's predestination, no will at all worth speaking of. The attack of F. Socin upon the Armenians produced a change in this doctrine, especially among Liberal Christian sects. Still neither of them can admit the free will of man and his inherent power for doing the good, without some qualification, or else they must deny the redeeming power of their Christ, inasmuch as there would be nothing left to be redeemed from. If my will is naturally potent enough to do the good, has perfect freedom to do it, and my reason enlightened by the Sinaic revelation, which is the common property of all men, guides me to distinguish correctly right from wrong, good from evil, and truth from falsehood,—I could not possibly be redeemed from anything by any faith, creed or church. If there is nothing to enslave me, I can not possibly be liberated. Therefore, every Christian must deny free will in order to be a Christian.

I believe I have fairly stated this "disagreement" between Jew and Christian. It centers in the idea of free will, freedom, which Judaism maintains without qualification, unless a man's crimes degraded him to brutality; and Christianity in all its various sects must either deny or so modify it that it ceases to be freedom in its proper sense.

It could not be my intention here to decide the question. I will only call your attention to the practical decision of the civilized world. Moral philosophy, as I believe I have stated in the introduction, can not build up a code of ethics on that particular dogma of the Church. If there were no freedom, there could be no accountability; there could be nothing in man's doings or omissions which is either positively good or bad, and the moral idea itself evaporates. Inasmuch as I am not responsible for that which God or Satan does through me, I am not a moral being, no free agent, there is no moral law in man; it is a mere issue between God and Satan, the causes and objects of which are unknown to man, who is a mere instrument, and no man could possibly build up a system of moral philosophy upon that basis. Therefore, the moral philosophers are under the obligation of rejecting that particular dogma of the Church, and to build upon the Sinaic theory of personal freedom and accountability, and the general moral government. If one or the other philosopher still calls his system of ethics Christian, and not Jewish, which it actually is by its substance, we can only imagine that he has unwittingly abandoned the dogma and returned to the Jewish aspect of morals as the primitive Christians did, whose conceptions, as to the incompatibility of the logical sequences of freedom and vicarious atonement, were imperspicuous and undefined. As far as moral philosophy is concerned, so much is certain, the civilized world decides in favor of the Jewish doctrine of freedom as the postulate of ethics.

As the practice is more important than the theory, the governments and legislatures of the civilized countries are more important than moral philosophy. The civilized countries the world over make and enforce laws on the principle of moral freedom and the accountability of every sane person of maturity, as though the dogmas of the Church had never existed. The law nowhere admits any criminal's plea, that Satan wrought the evil deed in him, who is but a tool, or that God predestined him for damnation, so he could not help committing crimes. No offender can justify his misdeeds before the law by the dogma, because the law is based upon the ideas of personal freedom and accountability. No government appoints, and no people elects judges or executors of the law under the supposition that the Holy Ghost will give them wisdom and rectitude, whatever they might have been or have done heretofore. Is that man fit for that position by the requirements of his reason and the uprightness of his will, as demonstrated in his antecedents? is the question to be answered entirely irrespective of the dogma. The question is, are his reason and will correct? which means free, energetic and enlightened, and not what does or will God or Satan do through him.

I do not speak of existing prejudices, more or less influential in this or that locality; I speak of the principle underlying all civil government and legislation; and this is freedom as the postulate of ethics, and not the dogma. Therefore, it must be admitted that the fundamental idea of constitutional government, the *Rechtsstaal*, is Jewish, as expressed in the Sinaic revelation, and not Christian, as advanced by St. Augustine, modulated by Thomas de Aquino or Duns Scotus, accepted by the Reformers and impressed on the creeds and catechisms. There is no medium between free and not free. Man must be one or the other. Moral philosophy and all modern governments decide the question in favor of Sinai. If it is not supposed that the vast majority of all reasoning human beings are predestined for damnation, it must be admitted that this very majority decides the question in favor of Freedom as the postulate of ethics, and we declare it decided on their responsibility.

IX.
PROVIDENCE AND THE DOGMA.

All thinking men necessarily agree that there is in or above this world of our cogitation a power superior to that of man individually and collectively. Naturalists call it Nature, fatalists call it Fate, scientists invented for it the terms Laws of Nature, pagans named it the Domination of the Gods, philosophers announce it as the Moral Government of the World (*die sittliche Weltordnung*), which is a mere definition of that sovereign exercise of the supreme power which all theists and religionists call Providence or the government of God in this concrete and visible world, the spiritual and moral doings of man. Every language of civilized people has a term or a phrase referring to man's dependency on Providence. The Bible contains the most various terms and phrases to express this idea. The Hebrews of Post-biblical days coined the Hebrew noun *Hashgachah* for Providence from a verb used in this sense in the Bible, and the popular phrase *Im yirtzeh hash-Shem*, "If it shall please God," which has found its way into all modern languages. The biblical term for Providence is *Adoni*, "Lord," which reappears in the Phœnician Adonis, and is a peculiar plural form of *adon*, "a human lord or master," to designate God as the sole sovereign of the world; God revealed in history. According to the Bible record, Abraham was the first man who called God *Adoni*. (Genesis xv. 2.) So it appears, he was the first to recognize the universal government of God, the Unity of Deity, as, according to Moses Maimonides, Abraham was the first who conceived the idea of the cosmos created by the ONE GOD, and therefore called him *Koneh Shamayim ve-Eretz*, "Possessor of heaven and earth" (Genesis xiv. 22), and also "Judge of all the earth." (*Ibid.* xvii. 25.) The same idea, in the form of Preserver, is expressed in God's name of *El-Shaddi*, with which, it is said, he made himself known to Abraham (Genesis xvii. 1 and Exodus vi. 3); while the idea of special Providence is expressed for the first time in the prayer of Abraham for the wicked people of Sodom and Gomorrah. The logical connection of these ideas is evident.

From Abraham to Moses the idea of special Providence predominates in the Bible record, because the history of the Abrahamitic family is its main subject. With Moses both aspects reappear in the only proper name of God, the ineffable JEHOVAH, the definition of which is given in Exodus

(iii. 14), "And Elohim said to Moses *Ehyeh asher Ehyeh*," etc., which signifies not merely I AM, but "I am the eternal being, essentiality and substance of all that is, was or will be," hence of all "Becoming," as the Hebrew verb *hayah* includes the two ideas of being and becoming, and the latter denotes a mere function of the former. In the same passage the divine voice commands Moses to go to the children of Israel and tell them *Ehyeh* (the first person), which signifies Jehovah (in the third person), "sendeth me to you," no tribal god and no special deity; the one, only Eternal and Sole God, as high and exalted, as profound and comprehensive or rather infinitely higher than human speculation can conceive Deity; and add thereto, the divine voice commanded, that this Jehovah is also the God of your fathers, Abraham, Isaac and Jacob, whom you know as *Elohim*, *Adoni* and *El-Shaddi*, the Creator, Governor and Preserver of the universe, the universal and special Providence.

All conceptions of tribal, local, special, tutelar or national gods of pagan speculation and modern reproduction fall to the ground, flat and dead, before this simple passage of two verses in Exodus. The idea is clear and evident. The Eternal Being, the cause and substance of all "Becoming," must necessarily be life and love, will and power, self-conscious intellect and sovereign wisdom beyond all knowable and thinkable perfection, as life, love, will and power, self-conscious intellect and wisdom are manifest in the perpetual "Becoming," in the eternal fitness of things, the beauty and harmony of nature, the teleological construction of living organisms, the functions and manifestations of all living creatures; and reason can not help admitting that there can be nothing in any effect which is not the cause thereof, and "Becoming" is the effect of "Being." If that is so, and none has ever been able to gainsay it successfully, then God must be manifest in every one of His creatures, as well as in the totality of his creation; his wisdom, goodness, power and truth must extend to the very lowest as well as the highest of His creatures: and thus He must be Providence, universal and special. So we are told that Moses knew the God of the fathers, and so he was commanded to announce and expound the ineffable One to Israel, so to be made known to all the children of man.

Permit me, ladies and gentlemen, to deviate for a minute from our subject, in order to remark that there is no positive atheist. There are atheists by levity, persons whose thoughts never reached beyond the sensual sphere, and whose vulgar motto is, I do not care. Another class of atheists is made by degradation, they want no God to take cognizance of their misdeeds and persuade themselves that there is none. Then come the atheists by the grace of their company. They happened to come in contact with atheists of any class, and being themselves incapable or too indolent to reason correctly and thoroughly, adopt their companions' theories. None of these classes can be called positive in their theories, as they do not rise from the source of logical thought. It is with them a mere aberration of a periodical nature. Scientists may become atheistical by the habit of expounding all phenomena on strictly mechanical principles or by the attempt of applying the laws of one science to all of them and to the science of sciences, a systematic understanding of the whole world (*Weltanschauung*). But none of them has become a positive atheist, if we are to believe their own confessions. Logical reasoners become apparent atheists by overthrowing the evidence of any theistical system, which means nothing positive; for that which overthrows may be overthrown. It is the particular abstract God of this or that philosophy, or the particular personal God of this or that theology, which, by its inherent defects, irritates reason to refute and then to deny it. In this case the reasoner may abide in the negation, if he be unable to conceive another idea of Deity than the one he refuted, and be an atheist, but only a negative one. Nobody has and none will construct a positive evidence that the existence of Deity is impossible, hence there is no positive atheist. I did not count the atheists by fashion, that are numerous in some localities, for they are everything only after a fashion, which is hardly worth while mentioning. Anyhow there is nothing positive in it. We return now to our subject.

With this knowledge of Deity, understood by Moses and comprehended more or less by the intelligent portion of the society about him, we leave the camp in the wilderness and approach Mount Sinai. There we hear *Anochi Jehovah Elohecho*, and we comprehend at once that this Jehovah is identical with the *Elohim*, whom we know to be the Creator, Governor and Preserver of the universe, the universal and special Providence of the universe and of every creature thereof, of this and every other nation, of this and every other individual. The very idea of revelation is, that Providence discloses its secrets to man to instruct him, that so the individual man must live and act his part on this stage of existence in order to reap the benefit in store for him in the bountiful lap of benign Providence. So the nation, so the nations must live and act their parts on the stage of history, obedient to the same code of ethics as the individual, in order to exist and prosper under the guidance of Him who shapes the ends and holds in His hands the destinies of the nations. If you, individual or nation, disregard and transgress the law of Providence, you by your own free will place yourselves outside of it, enjoy no longer its benefits, hence you are abandoned to luck, chance and casualty, you drift upon a boundless ocean of incalculable emergencies, and sooner or later, the impetuous billows of crushing casualties will overwhelm and crush you. You rebel against Providence and you forfeit its protection, you rebel against sovereign reason and you are abandoned to folly and absurdity, the illogical combat between man and physical nature. This is the sense of the twenty-sixth chapter of Leviticus, the ever returning refrain of which is, "If you will go with me in rebellion, I will go with you in the violence of rebellion." There are in this world two controlling forces for man, benign and wise Providence, unreasonable and heartless casualty; obey the law of Providence and live, abandon yourselves to casualty and perish. This is the fundamental idea of revelation, and history, with its blood-stained ruins and glory-crowned palaces, testifies to its truth. This is the doctrine of Providence, which can be defined and explained, analyzed and expounded, although nothing can be added to it, nothing can be taken from it. Calvary and Mecca have not changed it, the Reformation has not improved it, history in all its chapters testifies to it, you and I, all reviewing their mundane careers honestly and impartially, must confirm it. There is a Providence whose laws must be obeyed.

The main question, however, in this connection is, how does this definition of Providence agree with the principle of freedom which we know to be the postulate of ethics? Both being included in the same Sinaic revelation, they can not exclude one another. The next question suggesting itself is, by what means does Providence manifest itself to reach the human being or beings? These means must be intelligible to human reason or else we could form no idea of the workings of Providence. Well do we know the word of Scriptures, "He maketh the winds his messengers, flaming fire his ministers," and the remark in the Talmud, "Providence hath many messengers." But we also know something about the laws of nature and their stability. It is not so easy to believe that a steamer with hundreds of people on board sinks and all of them perish, because all of them were sinners, guilty unto death; or that a large city is destroyed by conflagration or inundation on account of the sinfulness of its inhabitants; or that a man walking on the sidewalk steps upon an orange peel, slips, falls and breaks a limb on account of his wickedness; or that this man is rich and happy on account of his merits and virtues, and the other is poor and wretched on account of his sins. So the balance of justice, it appears, is not so very correct as optimists, moralists and preachers maintain. Well we might say that these cases are exceptions to the rule, and the exceptions are very small, hardly more than necessary to establish the rule as such. But when we speak of special Providence in connection with the goodness and wisdom of the Almighty, it ought to reach every case. Let us take a closer survey of the matter, perhaps these questions are answerable.

In as far as Providence signifies the act of providing for the well being and prosperity of God's creatures, the energies of nature to produce abundantly for man and beast, the instincts of those creatures, and especially the reason of man to seek and gather in, are all sufficient to admit that this is a well-provided world. The combat for existence, or rather subsistence, is an enormous bubble, an imitation of affairs in a badly managed human society, which bursts at its first contact with reality; for in reality there is plenty for all and ten times more than the living beings on earth can possibly use. But if we speak not of that which we must have, but of what we wish and would like to have, that which is unnecessary to our well-being; and we find how partial Dame Fortune is in distributing her favors, how one must earn a bare livelihood in the sweat of his brow, while this railroad king, that banker, this merchant prince, that cunning speculator, this gambler, that robber, this swindler, that adventurer spends his years in frolicking and gayety, we must first accuse ourselves who yearn for things which we do not need, and then we must find fault with the organization of society which violates God's laws and stands in rebellion against the will of Providence to the very extent to which the cunning and successful individual deprives the laboring man of food, raiment and shelter. There must be a crime in the appetites of individuals and the government of society in exact proportion to the sufferings of a portion of its members; although wealth and high living are no conclusive evidence of happiness, as poverty and hard labor are no sure criteria of wretchedness. There are as many happy people in this world subsisting on scanty food, in hovels and coarse garments—yes, as many, and more than there are happy princes and millionaries. The thermometer with which to gauge human happiness is of a relative nature. The crime is in society, if by its inventions and contrivances, its ignorance and levity, accidents occur which cost the lives or health of human beings. Providence is correct and faultless; society is guilty of criminal neglect and ignorance. If we want to enjoy the advantages and benefits of our own inventions and ingenuity, which are the products of our own free will and reason, we must also take the risk of the mistakes and errors to which we are liable, and stand the consequences without an appeal to the mercy of Providence. In physical nature the laws of God are stable; man is gifted with reason and free will to know and use them to his advantage and prosperity, or misuse them to his own misery and destruction. The law of God is, reason correctly and act intelligently. This leads us into the *modus operandi* of Providence.

Notwithstanding all this and all that, there is a special Providence, and one which does not conflict with man's freedom. History testifies to the reign of universal Providence which shapes the destinies of nations, and nations consist of individuals; hence he who takes care of nations must also take care of the individuals thereof. We must, in order to understand it, bear in mind our definition of the term, which is taken from the words of the prophet Micha (vi. 8). Dogmatic speculations have led many away from plain truth, and prevented them from understanding the plainest statement. So when they say God is almighty, they define, " He can do what he wishes." You ask them, can God commit a folly? can God do the impossible? can He make any fact undone? and they must say no, and no again. Therefore, almighty signifies, God is the efficient cause of all beings, hence he possesses all the might; omniscience signifies, God knows all causes and their efficacy in the universe, and he is all-wise signifies, all consequences and all results of all efficient causes are evident to him. When we say God is omniscient it does not exclude the freedom of man, because the category of the probable is evidently not included in God's omniscience. If that carpenter ascends a rotten ladder to reach the roof, and the ladder breaks and the man sustains injuries, God's knowledge is not increased by that fact, which adds nothing to the contents of intelligence or reason. Where the law is known, single facts falling under that law do not increase the knowledge; hence it is not necessary that God, because He is perfect, should have the prescience of all particular occurrences within the bounds of probability, when He knows the totality of all possible probabilities. All discussions of God's prescience and man's freedom appear to have started from an erroneous conception of the two terms.

If the province of probability is in the power of man, he is free, and there it must be where God's special Providence is manifested. None, to my knowledge, has explained this point more clearly than Moses Maimonides. With Aristotle and the Peripatetics he admits that the laws of nature are the laws of Providence, which God changes not, because they are the perfect expressions of His will, wisdom and goodness, although He may momentarily interfere with them for the purpose of realizing particular aims in correspondence with His wisdom and goodness, for God is free. His law is his Providence in the realm of nature. The spirit of man, however, follows other laws, for the spirit is also free, and must be guided by other inherent laws. Hence God's special Providence exercises its influence in and through the spirit of man, as in the case of prophecy. As we stand physically in perpetual connection with this material world, so we stand spiritually in perpetual connection with the eternal spirit. Again as we are at liberty to increase or decrease our natural health and vigor, and become a better or worse receptacle for the benevolent influences of physical nature, or even reduce ourselves to a non-conductor and death; so in the spiritual realm we may elevate our spiritual nature by obedience to God's laws to the very height of human perfection, which we call nearness unto God, and so we may may degrade our spiritual nature by disobedience and rebellion to God's law to the low, and even the lowest condition, and be thus distant from the eternal Deity. Those who are near to God are better receptacles for the divine influence than those at a distance. Special Providence is identical with that influence upon the human mind, only that the better man conceives it better, and is thus partly rewarded for his goodness, and the evil-doer with the clogged reason and hardened heart conceives it more slowly or not at all, and is thus partly punished for his wickedness. It is through, and by the reason and mind of man that special Providence protects and guides him without any interference with his freedom, he being governed by his own inherent law.

If you wish to stand under the special protection of special Providence you must exert your energies to rise, to climb, to ascend and come as near to your God as you can, and conceive with ease the advice and counsel of the Ruler of man. If you neglect this, you expose yourselves to the freaks of casualty and the crushing wheels of fatalities. This is the eternal law, in perfect harmony with freedom and co ordination with the entire law of God. This is the doctrine of special Providence as proclaimed in the Sinaic revelation, to which nothing can be added, nothing taken away. This is the dogma of perfect harmony, of Providence and freedom which I have proposed to discuss this evening, and I am done. There is yet left to consider the nature of sin and atonement in connection with this dogma, which I propose to discuss in another lecture.

X.

SIN AND ATONEMENT.

The standard of rectitude is in human reason. That which we call conscience is an instinctive feeling of the human species that whatever is right ought to be done and whatever is wrong ought to be shunned, in consequence thereof righteousness is the cause of man's satisfaction and pleasure, and evil-doing is to him a source of dissatisfaction and pain. Conscience is, therefore, a universal human disposition, a characteristic which distinguishes him from the animal. Brutes have no conscience either in the deserts or forests of their original homes, or in their third and fourth generations in the zoological gardens, or in the farmers' stables. Among the lowest types of inferior races of men, the tenor note of conscience is discernible, although the conceptions of right and wrong differ widely among races, nations, tribes and individuals, because the definition thereof is the function and office of reason, which, being free, naturally varies, as the results of discursive reasoning generally do. This, however, does not affect the being of that innate disposition and feeling which we call conscience. It is there universally, so that no savage will maintain that he ought to do that which is wrong and shun that which is right in his consciousness. The cause then of the savage's low standard of morals is in the imperfect functions of his reason. As it is in the lowest stage of human development, so it must be in the highest and every intermediate stage, the primary cause is in conscience and the standard of rectitude is in human reason. For rectitude is the desire and determination to do that which reason decides to be right, and not to do the contrary thereof. The rabbis maintained, *Ain Am-ha-Aretz Chasid*, " the ignorant could not be a pious man," because his standard of rectitude must be as deficient as his reasoning. Jesus maintained that all sins may be forgiven except sins against the Holy Ghost, which, in the phraseology of those days, signifies the determined resistance against the enlightenment and correction of the reasoning faculty. Human reason in its state of perfection is the Holy Ghost of Christian and the *Ruach hak-Kodesh* of Jewish theology.

Imagine, now, that the souls of all shades of enlightenment be placed before the throne of sovereign justice occupied by the Omniscient Judge, who knows all doings of man and all motives thereof, all opportunities and facilities together with all hinderances and obstructions on man's path of life, and appeal to your reason for a decision, how must that Sovereign judge every one of those souls? The only proper decision, I think, must be that He judges every one according to his own standard of rectitude, in strict accordance with every man's conscience and consciousness, as said the prophet Jeremiah (xxxii. 19), and as in fact all prophets said, which led Rabbi Joshua ben Chananiah, another of the numerous Jesuses of that very age, in behalf of Israel to protest against the human arrogance of sectaries, who carry their intolerance into Heaven and impose it upon the eternal Deity, and to advance the idea which was formulated thus: *Chasidai Ummoth ha-Olam yesh lahem Chelek l'olam habba:* " Pious Gentiles (heathens, infidels, anybody) partake of life and bliss eternal." God judges every man according to his own standard of rectitude. The savage is right if his doings and omissions are in full accordance with his own standard of rectitude. The Jew, the Christian, the Mohammedan and every other man is right, if his doings and omissions are the dicta of his standard of rectitude. This piece of common sense, I believe, is generally admitted, except in the vulgar theology, although it is held that ignorance of the law is no excuse for crime. This is because we have a right to expect of every man in society to know the Ten Commandments, and crime actually signifies the transgression of any provision thereof. Ignorance is the original sin and stupidity the universal depravity, of which man must be redeemed. But this leads us to another point which we must premise.

The progress and happiness of society, hence also of every individual thereof, depends on the proximate perfection of the standard of rectitude. The proportion of happiness to that standard is believed to be exact. Man's innate yearning after happiness in connection with his conscience, the negative of which is his dread of pain, naturally prompts him to seek a higher or rather the highest standard of rectitude within his reach. It prompts his reason to seek the best and most reliable definitions of right and wrong. He seeks enlightenment for the sake of happiness. He longs after certainty to form his character and govern his volitions, to be sure of his being right before God and man. This is perhaps the noblest instinct of man and the best he can do, as none can reach perfection. To resist and neglect this instinct is a sin against human nature. It is spiritual suicide. Man is free, he may commit suicide, something which no animal can do; so may he suffocate in his soul also this purely human instinct and linger at the verge of self-dereliction. We are now prepared to define righteousnes. Righteousness is the ability or state of man to live and act in exact conformity with the highest standard of rectitude within his reach. The next and highest step of moral perfection is called holiness, which consists of delight in the good and true and repugnance to their opposite. The Sinaic revelation is premised with the divine promise, "And ye shall be unto me a kingdom of priests and a HOLY nation,," as the effect to be produced by the revelation. This is repeated by Moses especially in three passages (Leviticus xix. 2; xx. 26; xi. 44), to impress on the mind that personal holiness is one of the great objects of the Sinaic revelation, holiness by rectitude, by righteousness and by physical purity.

In his search after the standard of righteousness man encounters the difficulty of uncertainty. I do not know all, nor do I know best. Many men and certainly all men know more and better than I do. How, then, shall I know that I have fixed for myself the best standard of righteousness? No man of sound sense will deny this, hence every one must remain in a state of uncertainty on this important point. He appeals to human reason, to the experience of mankind crystalized in the religious and moral literatures of the world and in the laws of the different nations; he becomes more learned but not much wiser, for as in moral philosophy so in the laws the difference of principles is so marked that none can form from them a sure standard of righteousness, one which is certainly the highest within human reach. Therefore, Moses said to his people that the highest standard of righteousness, which will eventually lead you to holiness, to be a holy people, and the only one in which there is certainty on which you can rely, is not of human origin; it is in the Sinaic revelation which comes to you from the highest and immutable authority. Therefore, every honest and reasoning man, seeking the highest standard of righteousness, to form his character and to govern his volitions, so as to be right before God and man, will certainly seek it first and foremost in the sources of his religion, which he believes to be of divine origin. And if he succeeds not in finding it there, no all-just God can punish him for non-fulfillment of duty. Therefore, those ancient sages maintained that "Pious Gentiles partake of life and bliss eternal."

Please, ladies and gentlemen, permit me to interrupt this subject by a petition to those venerable men, who preach such a superabundance of Christian love for so little compensation, a petition in behalf of Jews and Gentiles, of four-fifths of the human family. Let me pray to them thus: Please let us have a share in God's grace, do not exclude us from the Father's house, do not monopolize altogether the love of Him who said, "I love you, saith Jehovah"; let us have some corner in Heaven, do not send us all *in corpore* to that bad place. Please do not prolong your line of intolerance to Heaven and eternity; it looks too unkind and too arrogant for any little man to degrade God to an arbitrary despot. If you do it not for the sake of the Father, do it for the sake of the Son, that he appear not so much smaller than that rabbi who formulated the Jewish doctrine, "Pious Gentiles partake of life and bliss eternal." And if you refuse to let us poor creatures go to Heaven, please let us live in peace here on earth. Do not flatter your customers that they are better men and better women than we are, because they believe in your extra doctrines, when the next moment you confess that they are all sinners after all. I will stop here and return to our subject.

After what we have said, it will be easy to define the term sin. The Sinaic revelation, building upon the postulate of freedom, admits that man may sin. It mentions three kinds of sin. For a sinner is he who is first wrong in his motives (*Avon*), secondly wrong in his action (*Pesha*), and thirdly wrong in the end or aim of his action (*Chatta'oh*). These are the very three terms in the revelation supplementary to the Sinaic (Exodus xxxiv. 7), and explanatory of one of its provisions. (*Ibid.* xx. 5.) We may say, then, according to the Sinaic revelation, that man is a sinner whose actions are prompted by evil motives, or whose actions are violations of his own acknowledged law of God according to his standard of righteousness, or also whose actions are productive of evil to others or even to himself. Wherever these three kinds of sin are combined in one action it is a crime. God punishes or forgives sins, and the Law punishes crimes. A sin, according to rabbinical definition, must be an action. The evil thought, some of them maintain, being actually negative only, as for instance unbelief, is not punishable with God, while the good thought, which is actually positive, is counted with the good deed. However, the Sinaic revelation ordains, "Thou shalt not covet," hence evil thoughts are identical with evil actions.

A person is not a sinner, because he committed one or more sins at different times, as is stated explicitly in Ecclesiastes (vii. 16-20). That writer comes to the conclusion that no *Tzaddik*, no righteous man, is without his sins. He becomes a *Rasha*, "a wicked man," if his general character is more inclined to acts of violence, sensuality and selfishness than to the right and good. So King David defines the term *Rasha* (Psalms xxxiv. 2-5; l. 16-20); so the rabbis of the Talmud and after them Maimonides in the code (*Teshubah*) understood it. We are, therefore, warranted in maintaining that he is a righteous man, *Tzaddik*, whose general character is formed and established in conformity with the highest standard of rectitude within his reach. The opposite thereof, *i. e.*, who seeks no standard of rectitude and cares for none, or he who has one and is not guided by it is a wicked man, *Rasha*.

It is evident from the Sinaic revelation that God forgives sins; because it is stated in only one particular case that God will not hold him guiltless who takes His name in vain, and it is plainly stated in the supplementary revelation (Exodus xxxiv. 7), " He forbeareth (or forgiveth) iniquity, transgression and sin,"· which is frequently repeated by Moses and expounded by the prophets in the plainest and most distinct language. It is also evident that none besides God can forgive sins, so we read (*Ibid.* xxiii. 20, 21) that the angel, messenger or prophet whom God promised to send before Israel in order to bring him to the land of promise, would not forgive their transgressions, although God's name or special authority was in him, which says plainly enough that this authority is delegated to none. Man is responsible to God and the law. Either of them may punish him for his misdeeds, and God alone can forgive them. Only in one case, it is said in the Decalogue, that God visits the iniquity of parents upon children to the third and fourth generations, and that is, as all Jewish expounders understood it, the iniquity of idolatry in him who knows that there is but one God, and from wicked motives worships others. Maimonides adds thereto that such a wickedness rooted in the head of a family, it may be supposed, will corrupt the whole of it. The third and fourth generations are mentioned, because, as in the case of Joseph (Genesis l. 23), so long a man might live and exercise that nugatory influence upon his family.

The principle, however, expressed in that part of the revelation appears to be, that the good and the true is imperishable in the history of the race; it bears perpetual fruit and perishes not in the memory of man; while all that is evil and false is doomed to perish in the next generation or in the third and fourth. This is a law of history as well as of revelation, well understood by the inspired men and the expounders of their words.

Everlasting punishment, eternal torments, the unquenched fire of hell, spiced with a dose of brimstone, and surrounded by a few teasing and triumphant devils, are the products of a rude northern imagination; the Sinaic revelation makes no suggestion of that kind. The whole is the product of a false speculation, a reasoning not from facts, but from prior conclusions. If sin means rebellion against the eternal God, its effect in Him must be eternal as He himself is, consequently the punishment must be also eternal. This is the foundation of that doctrine. But man's doings and omissions can only affect him and other men. They can no more affect God than I can affect the solar system by striking a blow upon a rock. God is perfect and immutable; man's doings and omissions can produce no change in Him. The Sinaic revelation speaks of a punishment to the third or fourth generations only; all prophets and all history confirm this; hence theologians had no right to invent that terrifying doctrine in order to frighten ignorant people into the lap of the Church, or to use it as a scarecrow for bearded children.

The means of atonement also are fully delineated in the Sinaic revelation. The people coming out of Egypt are considered to be in a state of sinfulness. (Psalms lxxviii. 22.) Moses announces to them the command of God, to prepare by various actions of sanctification for the great event, " For on the third day God will descend upon Mount Sinai in the sight of all the people." And the people did prepare as commanded. Prepare for what? To find and understand the loftiest and surest standard of rectitude. This is certainly the first step toward atonement, to prepare for the highest standard of rectitude within our reach; to feel convinced that we did not know hence, did not do right in the past, which arouses in every just man's heart sorrow, repentance and remorse, the hell fire in the human breast; and to long and yearn for higher and better knowledge.

And when the Israelites had received that highest standard of rectitude, they exclaimed :] *Na'aseh Venish'ma*—" We will do and will obey." This is the second step toward atonement, viz, now. that we are acquainted with the highest and surest standard of rectitude, we resolve and determine that we will be guided by it. So man returns to his God, so he obliterates his own sins, so he changes and reforms his character, so he rises to the dignity of manhood and enables himself to counterpoise and overbalance every misdeed of his by noble, generous and humane deeds; to extinguish the evil and replace it manifold by the happiness he brings to weeping humanity and to himself through others. This is the Sinaic system of atonement, corroborated by human reason and the facts of history and repeated by the prophets of Israel, especially by Isaiah (lv. 4–9) and Ezekiel (xviii.). The means of atonement, be they sacrifices according to Moses, or prayer, fasting and alms, according to the rabbis and many Christian teachers, are mere means to express the repentance, the remorse of the sinner, and his yearning after a higher standard of rectitude and the self-control to enable him to do right and to be right before God and man. The means change as man and his habits change, while the principle abides and endures forever. All dogmatic speculations and casuistic ordinances are worthless, if they run contrary to the principle, and are, in fact, but means for the time being.

We can not say that this exposition of doctrine concerning sin and atonement is one of our Agreements or Disagreements, for many Christian sects believe this doctrine, and only express it in other words and symbols, such as savior, baptism, faith, love, regeneration, second birth, and such other theological fictions, symbols to suggest ideas; while quite a number of Jews have resort to ascetic practices, like those Christians who kill or deaden the flesh, or the Hindoos who do it in fact, in order to appease the angry God and obtain of him atonement. One thing we know to a certainty, that this doctrine harmonizes with reason and is of Sinaic origin; hence, it rests upon the solid basis upon which no other fabric of salvation is built. It harmonizes with man's freedom, with the universal plan of Providence, with the goodness and justice of God; therefore, we believe in it.

XI.

IMMORTALITY AND SINAI.

The belief in the immortality of man's individuality or personality in any of the three forms of resurrection of the body, immortality of the soul, or both forms united, or transmigration of souls, connected with the idea of future reward or punishment or both, is so universal in the human family that a modern writer in Germany (*Der Seelencult von Julius Lippert*), with no small amount of learning, has attempted to prove by facts that man's belief in God or gods is based upon his prior belief in the immortality of the soul. The worship of departed ancestors, the attempts to please and win the favor of the good, to appease or banish the evil spirits, he thinks, led to the worship of God or the gods. Without attempting here any criticism on that theory, it must be admitted from the material compiled in its support, that the Grecian and Roman classical writers, who maintain that ancient Egypt was the country where the doctrine of personal immortality was first advanced and taught, were mistaken. They had no knowledge of the religions of China and India, none of the tribes and nations preceding the ancient Empires of Babel and Nineveh, of Syria and Palestine or of the Arabs. In fact their knowledge of man beyond Greece and Egypt did not even reach far into Ethiopia. Modern researches prove that the idea of personal immortality was universal among the ancient nations or tribes, whose theories and speculations have become known to us; and that the origin thereof is in gray pre-historical ages inaccessible to us now, so that, perhaps, none will ever be able to ascertain where and when it originated. It appears to be an innate consciousness of man that he is an immortal being, which, like the consciousness of freedom, duty, accountability and ideality in general, can be cultivated and perfected or obscured and extinguished by development or deterioration of human nature.

It makes no difference, however, whether the Egyptians or all other nations prior to Moses were in possession of the belief in immortality; it must be admitted anyhow that Moses and his cotemporaries must have been in possession thereof; whether they learned it in Egypt or their ancestors brought it with them from the land of the Chaldeans. This is, I think, admitted on all hands. And yet this amounts to circumstantial evidence only that the Hebrews in the time of Moses believed in immortality in this or that form. I think that there exists better evidence to this effect. Let us approach it by the way of history.

It is not necessary to search into the historic literature of the Hebrews after Josephus Flavius, as none doubts the existence of the belief in personal immortality among the Hebrews subsequent to that time. Josephus narrates (Antiquities xviii. I. 3; Wars II. viii. 11) that there existed in Palestine in the time of the Asmonean Jonathan, hence about 150 B. C., the three sects of Pharisees, Sadducees and Essenes. One point of dissension among them was the doctrine of immortality. The Pharisees believed in the resurrection of the body and immortality of the soul. The Essenes believed in the immortality of the soul only, with which, it appears, they connected the belief that good men after death become angels of different degrees, like Elijah who became the Angel of the Covenant or *Syndelphos*, or like Henoch, who became the Angel *Metathron*, the supreme scribe in Heaven, or both identical as the angel of prayer, mediator between God and man, the prince of the countenance, the prince of the world, upon which Paul based his Christology: and that the spirits of bad men become evil demons, as the belief was prevalent in the East, and is still in China and elsewhere. The Sadducees did not believe in resurrection, says Josephus, although it appears they had another form of belief in immortality different from the two other sects, as will be mentioned below. This record in Josephus proves beyond doubt that in 150 B. C. the doctrine of immortality was already so prevalent and old among the Hebrews that three sects quarreled over the form of the dogma.

Advancing one step higher up into antiquity we reach the Second Book of the Maccabees, which, being addressed to Aristobul, the tutor of the King (Ptolemy Physcos), must have been written at least two centuries before Josephus. We find in this book the martyr story of Hannah and her seven sons (chapter iv.), who die with the firm conviction and faith in immortality and future reward, and the same doctrine is forcibly announced and emphasized in many other passages of the book. (II. Maccabees iii. 1; v. 15, 18; vi. 18; xii. 43; xv. 12 and elsewhere.)

One step higher, and we reach that very eminent book, called Wisdom of Solomon, which is apocryphal according to Jews and Protestants, and canonical according to Catholics. In my opinion it was written in Palestine by the same Aristobul, as a general introduction to his Commentaries of the Bible which he wrote for that Ptolemy. This book is a sort of Gospel of immortality, in which life eternal, future reward and punishment are made the rock and center of ethics and the final cause of this mundane life.

One step higher again, and we stand before Daniel, Ecclesiastes and Job, in which no unprejudiced reader can overlook the frequent expressions given to the immortality doctrine, reward and punishment hereafter. Then we come to Ezekiel (chapter xxxvii.) and much higher up to Isaiah (chapters xiv.; xxv. 8; xxvi. 19) and to the Psalms (xvii. and xlix.), and find the doctrine of immortality generally known, understood and believed in Israel. The Books of Kings and of Samuel especially lead up to David and Samuel with perfect certainty. The Witch of Endor could not have conjured up the spirit of Samuel, and he could not have said to Saul, "Tomorrow thou and thy sons will be with me," if immortality was not the general belief among the Israelites. This story leads us clear back to the Law of Moses. For the Witch of Endor is called in the text *Ba'alath Ob*, Mistress of Ob, or one skilled in conjuring up the souls of the deceased to reveal certain secrets, a mystic art which Saul had attempted to extinguish in Israel in obedience to the Law of Moses, which prohibits expressly and emphatically all species of those mystic arts (Deuteronomy xvii. 9–11), one of which is communion with the souls of the deceased or vulgar spiritualism. Why should Moses have prohibited this mystic practice, if it was not prevalent among his people; and how could such manipulations find credence among the people, if it did not believe in personal immortality and conscious existence after death?

Led back to Moses by a historical chain and with the circumstantial evidence recited before, we find also in the Pentateuch quite a number of passages testifying to the prevalence of that belief in the time of Moses and prior thereto. At the very threshold of man's history, we find in Genesis that man was CREATED (*bara*), as heaven and earth were CREATED, and as was animal life. Only in these three instances the text speaks of creation, in all other instances of original production other terms are used, such as he said, he made, or he formed. This distinguishes man as a third and separate creation. This, according to the sacred text, refers not to the body of man, which was made of the dust of the ground, but to the *Tzelem*, which made of the body of clay a man. (Genesis i. 27.) "And Elohim created man by his *Tzelem*." This term is defined in the second chapter to be the *Nishmath Chayim* (verse 7), by which the body of clay became a living man; and this was a new creation. This "Breath of Life" or soul of life or life soul, is not a thing which was dead or material at any time. It is not taken from the elements which might be destroyed. It is not an organism which is subject to dissolution. That *Tzelem*, by which man is in likeness with God, is the *Nishmath Chayim*, the life-soul, blown into his nostrils by and from the Almighty himself; hence a something which never was dead and is not subject to the dominion of death. So almost all Jewish commentators understood those passages in Genesis, which announced man from the very beginning as a being consisting of a body of clay and a deathless soul. Therefore they called the soul *Chelek Eloha mim-ma'al*, " the portion of God from on high," and like him not subject to death, the formative principle which ceases not to exist, when the form it produced be broken and destroyed.

This dualism returns again and again in the Pentateuch. When Rachel died, Scripture narrates, " And it came to pass when *her soul went away* (or out) when she died." Death is described in this case as the departure of the soul from the body, not as the end of life. When Jacob died (Genesis xlix. 33) we are told that " he was gathered unto his people," or he went home to his ancestors, exactly as all ancient nations with ancestral cultes paraphrased the death of their venerated fathers. Here the idea of meeting his ancestors in heaven is clearly expressed. When Moses sang, " This is my God and I will adore Him, the God of my fathers and I will extol Him " (Exodus xvii. 2), he did certainly not mean the dead ancestors, that exist no more and could have no God; he meant the immortal ancestors who live under the protection of Him, who was also his God, as both Jesus of Nazareth and Rabbi Gamaliel understood it, that He is not the God of the dead, He is the God of the living. When that same Moses furthermore exclaimed (Deuteronomy xxxii. 39), " See now, that I, I am He and no *Elohim* with me; I kill and I enliven, I crush and I heal, and none can deliver from my hands; for I lift up my hand to Heaven (Almighty), and I have said, I live forever"; he could only think of life after death and healing after being crushed and added, therefore, the assurance, that God is almighty and life eternal. He must have thought the same when he prayed (Psalms xc. 3), " Thou turnest man to dissolution (not contrition), and sayest, return ye sons of man." David based upon this idea his beautiful expression (Psalms xvi. 10), " For thou abandonest not my soul to Sheol, thou sufferest not thy pious ones to see corruption."

It is one of the errors of speculative theology that it attempted to bandage the eyes of Scripture readers, so as not to see how the Old Testament is full of expressions to prove beyond a doubt that man's personal immortality always was in Israel a universal and established belief, although neither Moses nor the prophets based upon it their system of ethics and divine worship, the reason of which was very plain, and was expressed by the prophet, " No eye besides thine, O God, hath seen it, He hath made it to wait for him"; and the rabbi has expressed it thus, " Be not like servants who serve the master for the sake of reward; be like servants who serve the master not for the sake of reward, and let the fear of Heaven be upon you." Base your canon of ethics and worship upon the immortality foundation, and you will soon discover that this belief, being a belief and hope only, could never be so firmly established, that none could doubt, all know and understand it; consequently in this case, all men who fail to know and believe, to understand and comprehend this one fundamental doctrine, lose their moral hold, the very object of all morality and piety; and so you destroy the very canon of ethics and worship.

Base your canon of ethics and worship upon the immortality idea, and you have made of it a system of selfishness, that is, you have made morals immoral and worship, blasphemy. You only do what you do and say what you say for the wages you expect to receive. You make of ethics a garment to keep you nice and warm, and of worship a sort of savings bank in which to deposit your spare pennies for future use.

Base your canon of ethics and worship upon the immortality doctrine, and you move the center of gravity from this into another world. You make of this life a mere caravansary, where we stop a little while to procure food for the long journey through an unknown wilderness. The consequence of such a teaching, which none could observe better than Moses could in Egypt, is that men care not for this world and this life, their fate and their progress, and become indolent slaves, if the right man comes to subject them and domineer over them. If a man's interest is not in this life and this world, he, of course, can not care much about either, and can not possibly be such a citizen of a commonwealth or such a member of the human family as Moses proposed man should be, free, just, humane and useful.

After all, we could not possibly know more of life eternal than that it is a continuation of life here, a prolongation of the same straight line, a steady advancing from lower to higher states. We can arrive there only as we prepare ourselves here. No man has a right to expect more than his desert. Justice can not grant more, and grace is of the same wisdom with justice. The object of ethics and worship is to unfold, cultivate, enrich and ennoble your soul in this world, and to hope for that world which he has made "to wait for Him." Bishop Warburton might have taken these points into consideration.

Base your canon of ethics and worship upon the simple foundation of the elevation, progress and perfection of man and mankind, as Moses did, a foundation which none can deny or doubt, and you reach the proper end of human happiness here and hereafter without subjecting your system to the objections just discussed.

Theologians have so long maintained the absurdity that the common men repeated it thoughtlessly, and extended it to all Hebrews of all ages and zones. Thus "the Jews believe in no eternal life." It is strange that the Jews themselves know nothing of that denial, as is evident from what we have stated already, and becomes self-evident from their theological and traditional literatures. All Jewish exegetics, metaphysicians and philosophers up to Philo and Aristobul, of Alexandria, up even to the translators of the Septuagint, maintain and expound the doctrine of immortality as purely Jewish doctrine. Again all traditional and rabbinical writings, from beginning to end, represent the belief in future life, reward and punishment as a doctrine of Jewish revelation. In the Talmud and its preceding books, as well as in every catechism, this belief is announced and emphasized. Hundreds and thousands of books on this subject, some full of absurd superstitions, have been written on the subject. The Kabbalists and mystics have depicted heaven and hell in as lively a manner as the most successful Methodist preacher, only with a little more Oriental imaginatian. The Jewish prayer-books are full of it, and the principal and simplest one of all, the *Mechalkel Chayim* of the Daily Prayers, " Thou sustainest the living in grace, thou revivest the dead in abundant mercy," etc , is believed to have been composed by the men of the Great Synod in the time of Ezra. The very fact that Jesus and his apostles taught the doctrine of immortality in the same form as the Pharisees did, ought to be proof positive that a belief in immortality was in Israel prior to the advent of Jesus; or rather he would not have taught immortality if he had not found it in Israel.

The most telling, perhaps, and also the strangest passage in this connection is that ancient Mishnah in Sanhedrin, " And these are the persons who have no share in life to come, he who denies that the resurrection of the dead is taught in the *Thorah*, who maintains there is no *Thorah* from Heaven, and the Epicurean. This points to the person who denies resurrection, revelation, and the existence of Deity, as did the Epicureans. But it says, besides, that one must believe, immortality or resurrection is taught in the *Thorah*, by Moses, we might say, and this is the strange point in that passage. It shows that all Jews, or at least all Pharisees and Essenes, believed that Moses did teach immortality; against which, and not perhaps against immortality itself the Sadducees protested. The word " Epicureans" for atheists point back to the time before the Maccabees, to the dissensions between *Hassidim* and Grecians when Epicureans existed in Israel. The other part of the passage also points to that time, when revelation was denied and immortality was believed on the authority of Socrates, Plato and other philosophers, but not on the authority of revelation. This is partly corroborated by a well-known passage in *Aboth* of Rabbi Nathan, which brings up the schism of the Sadducees among the doctors up to the school of Antigonos, hence to the first half of the third ante-Christian century, after it may have been an old question among all other classes of people.

Jesus knew this doctrine and adhered to it. When the Sadducees asked him that known question about the future world, he answered them in go d Pharisean language, that in the future world men will have no physical bodies, no corporeal passions, no bodily wants. "The righteous will sit with their crowns upon their heads and enjoy the splendor of the She-kinah," the Pharisees add. But after Jesus had fully answered the question of the Sadducees, he continues to prove this doctrine homiletically from a passage in the *Thorah* (Matthew xxii. 31, 32), exactly as Rabbi Gamliel did. Why this second and superfluous explanation? He wanted to prove that immortality or resurrection is taught in the *Thorah*, by Moses we might say, as all orthdox Israelites then believed.

Where and how is it taught in the *Thorah?* That Mishnah passage answers the question in full. Why does one deny resurrection or immortality in the Thorah? Because he denies divine revelation. Why does he deny this? Because he denies God. The three ideas are logically connected and arranged in that Mishnah. Invert the order and you must say, he who believes in God and in divine revelation, must necessarily also believe in the personal immortality of man as being announced in that very *Thorah*. The fact that the eternal God revealed His will to man, is the guarantee and proof of his immortality. Imperishable wisdom can not be addressed to perishable nature, as little as man can teach moral philosophy or theology to the dumb animal, although it may understand articulate sounds. The spirit only can understand the spirit, and the spirit can not perish, since it is of God, and not of matter; it is simple and not organic, hence not subject to dissolution. The Sinaic revelation is the *Thorah* in which immortality or resurrection is taught by divine authority to all Israel, which was to demonstrate that all are immortal beings, and not the select ones, as was the belief in Egypt, India, Athens and Rome; all are God's children, born and destined for immortality. Therefore, after the Sinaic revelation the people exclaimed, " This day we have seen that God speaketh to man, and he liveth" (Deut. v. 11), he is immortal, for he can understand God's speech. The announcement and the evidence of immortality is in the Sinaic revelation. No more announcement was necessary, and no better evidence could be given. Therefore, certainly Moses and Israel knew and believed this doctrine, as all must forever do who believe in revelation. This is in brief what I have to say on the subject of " Immortality and Sinai." The argument based thereon will be the subject of my next lecture. The revelation is, in the first place, the most convincing proof of the dominion of the spirit and its sovereignty over matter and its modifications. It is in the second place the evidence for the similarity in kind of the divine and the human spirit. It is in the third place the demonstration of the perpetual relation of the individual to the universal spirit, as the body stands in relation to matter. Therefore, it is *per se* the most expressive lesson of personal immortality and its best evidence.

XII.

A RESUME OF THE BODY OF DOCTRINE.

The Body of Doctrine is a technical expression to denote an aggregate of doctrines or fundamental theories logically connected, which form the basis of any system of religion or ethics. I have attempted in the previous lectures of this series to analyze the doctrines contained in the Sinaic revelation. This Body of Doctrine is fundamental to the three religions of Judaism, Christianity and the Islam. However widely doctors may disagree in definitions and subordinate points, they must agree in the main, viz: that this is the substance of what is called positive or revealed religion; hence we have set forth the "Agreements," and merely pointed out some "Disagreements" in regard to definitions and subordinate points.

We agree that this is not a world of dead matter, with mechanical forces, irrational, insensible, cold and dead, thoughtlessly and aimlessly engaged in perpetual production and destruction. Neither Monism nor Atomism, neither Evolution, in as far as it is a mere conglomeration of mechanical principles and hypotheses without foundation in fact, nor Positivism, with its agnostic basis and its method of selecting facts of experience or experiment as the only knowable truth, can satisfy us who believe in the existence of consciousness and reason, freedom and love, the intelligence of the human family, and the spirit which must be the substance of which all these functions are accidents or qualities. Like the Preacher of old we feel necessitated to exclaim over all those systems which, like the wind, come and go, "Vanity of vanities, all is vanity and windy thought." We can not adopt them as fabrics of thought, because they negate consciousness, freedom and reason; nor can we believe in them as a matter of faith, since they are hostile to the moral and emotional nature of man. Therefore, whether Jew or Gentile, believer or skeptic, we must seek refuge in the underlying fact of the world's theology, to protect ourselves and others against pessimism, misanthropism, despair and suicide, which are the natural and actual offspring of sophistry, fallacy and falsity. Daily experience confirms this dolorous fact. "The wicked flee when none pursueth and the righteous rest secure like the Lion." (Proverbs xxviii.) The world's civilization and the happiness of the individual enjoyed therein were not erected upon the systems of the godless; they have never achieved any great triumphs in the cause of humanity. Society and its institutions rest upon the fundamental idea of the spirit, the One and Eternal God. At this advanced age of the human family we can not begin history anew, nor dare we risk happiness and progress upon individual speculations. We can not say to all history, thou art wrong, nor is it either just or sensible to advise our neighbor, who dwells in security in his own house, to leave it and roam over boundless wastes without approved guide or compass. Therefore we must come to the same conclusion as did the Preacher of old, "At the end of the thing all is to be heard : Fear God and keep His commandments, for this is the whole man," the whole guide and compass of man.

This belief in the One and Eternal God led us into the truism of the perpetual connection of individual and universal spirit, the connection of man with God ; as in physical nature also the individual being stands in perpetual connection and reciprocity with the cosmos. Therefore revelation as a psychological fact is as natural as the process of digestion and assimilation as a physical fact. The one is even as necessary as the other to him who believes in the unity or oneness of God, as demonstrated by the unison of nature. The most momentous of all supposed direct manifestations of the universal to the individual spirit appeared to us in the Sinaic revelation, because it contains in substance all the doctrine and law necessary for man and mankind to secure to themselves salvation, peace and happiness here and hereafter, the life of righteousness in time and its just reward in eternity. Although as reasoners we must reject the evidence of miracles, we can not risk the happiness of man to a frail craft made of supernatural or even unnatural allegations, and our Maker has granted us freedom of thought; yet we can not deny the Sinaic revelation, on account of the historical evidence in its support ; the evidence of an entire nation and its uninterrupted traditions, the evidence of all Israel from the very day when he stood before Jehovah at Horeb to this last quarter of the nineteenth century; the evidence of all Christian and Mohammedan believers of all centuries, generations, climes and zones, whose very fabrics of religion, law and government, aye, the fabric of civilized society, are based on this very belief in the Sinaic revelation as a direct manifestation of Diety to man. In the face of this historical evidence it matters not whether we are able to understand the fact or whether it is beyond the horizon of our cogitation, we are bound to believe that which is historically authenticated and we have no means to contradict.

Next we analyzed the substance of the Sinaic revelation and found in it the elements of human knowledge to direct and guide him safely, the individual and the community, to human perfection and happiness. The jurist acknowledges in this revealed substance the foundation of right, the divine authority of justice, and the categories of law, to which nothing can be added and from which nothing can be taken away. So we find in it the highest and surest standard of rectitude to lead the nations to justice, peace, freedom, equality, prosperity and happiness; to guide the individual to righteousness and holiness, satisfaction and happiness, the formation of firm and solid character in consonance with the will of God and the happiness of man, and the preparation for eternal life and felicity. We find in the Sinaic revelation the highest species of evidence affirming and establishing in the mind of man the existence and love of the Eternal God, the godlike nature and immortality of man, the reality of the moral law, the dominion of God's universal and special providence, the freedom of man and his accountability to God and the Law, the mercy of our Heavenly Father for the repentant sinner, the perfectability of human nature and the solidarity of the human family with one God, one justice, one freedom and one love for all. This is the Body of Doctrine with its sufficient reason contained in the Sinaic revelation. These are the elements of human knowledge, together with the adequate motives to elevate man and mankind to that high position of satisfaction and happiness which is the ideal of all philanthropists.

So far we have remained within the bounds of our " Agreements." No fair reasoner will deny an iota thereof. Those who feel the woes of humanity and sympathize with the afflicted and oppressed must accept this Body of Doctrine as the elements of salvation. Those who speak of the religion of the future man can not help confessing that whatever is established in the nature and reason of man will remain with the race forever; therefore, in as far as this Body of Doctrine is established in the nature and reason of man, it will be the religion of all generations, as we have no cause to doubt the final and universal triumph of truth over all superstition and sophistry, and no cause to think that there could exist a religion without God and revelation, and the doctrines which are the logical sequents thereof. In as far then as Judaism is the religion revealed on Sinai, it is the universal religion, and must become the religion of the future man. Truth once enunciated remains truth forever. It is not changed or improved by any progress in science or art, any number of inventions or discoveries. The truth established on Mount Sinai remains truth forever.

But there are also " Disagreements," and there the tribal religion, the sectional religion, the exclusive religion, the intolerance and fanaticism begin. Some people, both Jews and Gentiles, believe too much, and are eager and zealous that others also should believe like them; there the strife begins. We all believe in one God. We are monotheists. All worship God as the loving father of man. The more intense and correct this belief the more tolerant and charitable man ought to be toward his fellow-man, also the erring and wicked, who, after all, is the child of the same Father of all. The "Agreements" produce harmony. But there comes to it the element of "Disagreement," and produces intolerance and fanaticism. Wherever the Jew maintained that God was only the God of Israel and the patron of Palestine, or imagined Him in the anthropomorphous form, a mighty king sitting upon a lofty throne in His heavenly palace, surrounded by a host of ministering angels, engaged exclusively with the affairs of His chosen people, he became a fantastic fanatic, and his religion tribal, narrow and intolerant. He must go to Palestine to find his God, and must have his own country and government, for this world is not God's world with him. Confused and defective reasoners still fancy a Jewish nationality and government, the restoration of the throne of David under a Messiah king, of which there is no idea in the Sinaic revelation or the laws of Moses. They despair of human reason and the progress of humanity, the solidarity of mankind and the advancement toward that objective point of all prophecy, because their conceptions of God and His government are inadequate obscured and confused; because they disagree with Israel, whose God is the Creator, Preserver and Governor of the universe and the merciful Father of mankind. They disagree with Israel, and there begins their "Disagreement" with the world and its affairs.

When the Mohammedan limits the infinite Deity to his own mosques and confines God's eternal love and mercy to his few co-religionists whose faces are turned in prayer toward Mecca; when he condemns to eternal misery all infidels, *i. e.*, all non-Mohammedan human beings, and imposes upon the God of freedom the Oriental Heathen fatalism, he establishes his "Disagreement" with the rest of mankind, misconceives the Eternal God, excludes himself from the family of man, disregards the affairs of this world makes, himself a subservient slave, and becomes a fanatic whose sole objec- of existence is to enter the Mohammedan paradise, although his practice widely differs from his theories, as is often the case also among other people. His fundamental error is in his misconception of the Eternal Deity.

And now comes the orthodox Christian sectarian and tells you that all your doctrines may be true and good, but they are worthless unless you believe also in the dogmas of Christology, the first point of which is the belief in a triune God. If you urge the right of reason to reject whatever is hostile to its dicta, contrary to first principles; he will answer you with the *credo*, you must believe it just because you can not comprehend, not understand, not think it, because it is a contradiction in its very terms, it is a mystery, a matter of faith, and faith signifies to believe contrary to reason. You must renounce and sacrifice reason to receive the reward of faith, for without this special reward you are damned and lost. It is this very precept which always made and makes now so many schismatics, infidels and atheists. They take the God of dogmatic theology as the God in fact and reality, and find it easy to dethrone and deny it.

If you furthermore urge, that if an inexplicable mystery it be, it could be made true and sure only by a divine revelation; for what man can not understand he could not possibly advance as a fact, unless he obtained his knowledge thereof by undoubted sensual impressions or by eye-witnesses whose veracity and capacity he could not doubt. Neither of which can be the case in the human knowledge of God's nature and essentiality. In revelation, however, throughout the old Bible and its Apocrypha there is no idea of a trinity; and according to some of the best expounders of the New Testament it is not there. It was not even an established belief of the Church prior to the Council of Nice, and right there and after it the protests of prelates were loud and emphatic against it. Hence it was certainly not a revelation, which in so important a point must have been at least as clear and intelligible as was the first revelation: "I, Jehovah, am thy God," which it was to contradict or supplement. If it is no revelation, how could I know and believe it? Especially, if I know that trinitarianism is taken from the Pagan shrine, why must I believe in it?

To all this, however, your trinitarian friend will reply somewhat to this effect: I accept the canonical books of the New Testament as a new revelation, and have no doubt in the perfect truth of its statements. There are, however, passages in that New Testament, especially in the Gospel, according to John, and also in the Epistles of Paul, Jesus speaking of himself or being spoken of by John or Paul in a manner which I can understand only to the effect that he was an incarnation of the Deity himself. So do I find in the same book passages which refer to the Holy Ghost as a separate being or another manifestation of the same Godhead. Unable to understand those passages otherwise, I must either believe in three Gods or one God who consists of three persons. Being a Monotheist, as according to the Synoptics Jesus certainly was, and according to the other Epistles his Apostles also were, I am obliged to be a trinitarian and believe in one God in three persons.

This argument, you see, is fair enough, but it rests upon the point that because there are certain passages in the New Testament which might be explained by the trinitarian hypothesis, therefore the Supreme Being must be in fact a triune God. Others, and Christians, too, explain those passages differently, hence there is no certainty in them. Others, again, advance that a hypothesis contrary to first principles, is illegitimate, whatever it might explain. So, for instance, one might advance the hypothesis that the authors of the New Testament writings were guided by Philo's speculations and Pagan beliefs, and glorified their master with poetical tropes taken from those sources. Hypothesis against hypothesis is good argument, especially if the latter is not contrary to first principles, and the former is. But the argument is faulty in itself. The hypothesis could only establish the possibility of understanding those passages in that manner; it can never establish the fact that God is, or is not, a triune being. Confess at once that there are certain passages in the New Testament, as there are quite a number in Revelations of John, Daniel and elsewhere, which you do not understand, and perhaps nobody else ever will be able to understand them, the historical key to unravel the mysteries having been lost; and be guided by first principles in harmony and unison with human reason.

So you might go on arguing for days, perhaps for weeks, and neither the trinitarian nor the unitarian would be exhausted, and at the end, most likely, each would believe as he did before; because they agree in principle, viz: in their belief in one God, and disagree only in the understanding of certain passages in this or that holy book, which perhaps both of them misunderstand.

The rabbis of old maintained that a belief in dualism or trinitarianism, especially if inherited of the fathers, is not to be considered Paganism, and so does Joseph Albo treat the question in his book "On Principles"; because the Dualist or Trinitarian does not deny the one God: he merely assumes another definition of the term. Definition is the office of reason, and reason is free before God and man. The same is the case with the Mohammedan and the Jewish Kabbalist and Anthropomorphist, as Moses Maimonides often expressed it. The Living God of Israel, the Almighty, Preserver and Governor of the Universe, is the principle which guides and pervades Jews, Christians and Mohammedans. The "Disagreements" are in the definitions, as is the case also in conscience. Those who attach to their definitions the value of essentiality and the importance of principle, become intolerant fanatics who have so often disturbed the peace of the human family, and tear it apart in hostile factions and exclusive clans. Rational men, fair reasoners, are humble and tolerant, and understand well that we possess only two authorities to decide those questions, the one of which is reason, which can not go beyond first principles, and will never attach undue importance to its own definitions; and the second is the Sinaic revelation, which teaches us that God is, and what He desires man to do and what to be. It is not in man's power to know *what* God is, hence we know only the announcement: " I, Jehovah, am thy God "; if he was a triune God, we could not possibly know it; it is not in reason, it is not in revelation; it is not necessary to know it. If it were, I think and believe

God would have told us somewhere and somehow, I, Jehovah, am a triune God.

You see, all we can do and ought to do is, that we agree to disagree in such issues, while we agree in principle. This great republic was built up, and is governed on this very principle, and the experiment has proved a success. Let us learn and apply the lesson of experience. Let us humbly and patiently wait till mankind shall be advanced far enough to decide its "Disagreements." The time will come as sure as the day succeeds the night. Until it comes let us live together in peace and good will.

XIII.

PARADISE, HELL, SATAN, EVIL SPIRITS OR RECOMPENSE.

Eschatology, as the theologians call the doctrine of the last and final things, the judgment after death, the resurrection of the dead and the last judgment day, including the various modes of punishment or reward in another region of the universe or on this earth radically changed for the resurrected man; eschatology engaged the minds of the theologians and philosophers of all ages, among Pagans as well as among Israelites, Christians and Mohammedans. This, according to its nature, being a matter of faith and speculation exclusively, without any basis of cogitable facts, imagination found in it a wide scope to build up conditions and states of happiness or misery, of entity or nonentity, which were grasped by faith and rendered acceptable by speculation.

Imagination is lawless reason. It is a free function of the mind. None can foretell its productions, as it is subject to no law. The countless varieties of dreams, of melodies in music, of stories, sceneries and figures of speech in poetry, and the variegated productions of fancy in all other fields bear testimony to its perfectly lawless freedom. Therefore, in eschatology, which offered so boundless a field to fancy, the views and doctrines, the hopes and fears, the promises and menaces are of infinite variety among theologians and philosophers.

· One point, however, is strange in this connection, and it is this: If you run over the Talmud and *Midrash* of the Hebrews, you will be astonished to find in them precisely the same views, doctrines, phantasma and phantoms as in the New Testament and its Apocrypha, in the Fathers of the Church and the Koran and its expounders. Consequently the speculations of the reflective minds on those topics are about the same among the different writers who adhered to any of the three creeds. Also the recent speculations of Protestant theologians about the nails, hair and intestines of the resurrected men have their counterpart in the Talmud, in the question earnestly discussed there, whether the righteous will rise with or without their garments, with or without the bodily blemishes, diseases and deformities of their mundane life. All the materialistic conceptions of the future state and judgment up to the purely idealistic *Visio Dei essentialis*, " to enjoy the luster of the Shekinah," as the Jews expressed it, as you find them in Christian theology, the Heavenly Jerusalem included, you meet them in the Talmud. The Jews, therefore, found, as regards this matter, as much satisfaction in their Talmud as did the Christians in their New Testament and dogmatic theology and the Mohammedans in their Koran, with the exception of the female attendants on the saints in Paradise.

It would be very interesting to compile the eschatological statements of the Talmud, and place them in juxtaposition to those of the New Testament, the Koran and their various expounders. It would prove, I think, that all of them, including the resurrection and ascension of the Christian Savior and his descent to Hades, were borrowed from the Jews; productions of fancy by different men in different climes and ages can not be as identical as those allegations are; and the rabbis of old, distant as they were from Rome as far as Persia up to India, could hardly be supposed to have borrowed of Christian theologians, although they did adopt Pagan myths and Judaized them. The miracles also, the apparitions and ghost stories are of the same kind and intent in all those sources, and the reasoning of later theologians runs over precisely the same ground among Jews, Christians and Mohammedans. But our time and space would not permit us to undertake that interesting work. We can only say here that the Jews believed, like Christians and Mohammedans, in future existence, reward and punishment on exactly the same ground of alleged facts, long before the philosophers took up the dogma, reasoned on the subject, and rendered it acceptable to the reasoning mind, long before Pythagoras and Socrates, long before Zoroaster and Confucius, too, because the consciousness of immortality, like the knowledge of the existence of God, is man's heritage from Heaven. All the legends and myths which were invented to represent this belief in an acceptable garb amount to no more than a proof that the consciousness of immortality was in man long before he philosophized. It is not the product of discursive reasoning; it is man's own birthright; it is part and parcel of his nature.

Some of these legends and myths refer to his Satanic majesty, the prince of darkness, Lucifer, Mephistopheles, the vulgar Devil, with his host of little devils, evil demons, unclean spirits, whose chief abode is in some unknown place, called Gehenna, Gehinnom, Hades, purgatory, hell, Abaddon, and five other names, according to the Talmud. That bad place, of course, is dark, dismal and cold, although a perpetual fire of brimstone burns there, in which the wicked souls are burnt, purified or forever tormented. It must be a cold and dark fire, and yet it burns and torments the poor souls in that cold and dark place. Imagination in various ages and localities depicted those *Dramatis Personæ*, and peopled that dreadful palace with phantoms in correspondence to the tastes, grossness of crimes, the ignorance and stupidity of the vulgar masses, to which priests and schoolmen added their shares, as the nurse shaped her tales and the school-master bound his rod according to the rudeness and wickedness of the parents whose children were intrusted to their care.

It is unnecessary, perhaps, to say now, at this high noon of enlightenment, that those stories, legends and myths are products of fancy without any foundation in fact; and deserve no more credence than the stories of the same kind in ancient mythology or in the demonology of China. Everybody almost knows now that which a rabbi in the third Christian century said, "All the prophets prophesied concerning the days of the Messiah," which signifies the future of the human family on earth; "but concerning the coming world (the state of existence hereafter) 'No eye hath seen it besides thee (God); He hath made it to hope (or wait) for him.'" No human intelligence can understand a state of existence purely spiritual, hence none could approximately define the nature of spiritual reward or punishment, or of a place where the souls of the departed abide. It is all speculation based on speculation, and imagination taking its material from this mundane life, with its fears and sufferings. It is evident, therefore, that all which has been written on Satan, evil spirits, Gehenna or Paradise, purgatory or hell, fire and brimstone, is poetry, plain and simple, without any solid fact to rely upon or any principle of reason to defend it. These things belong to the museum of antiquities, to the arsenal of history as characteristics of the ages and places, where those respective legends and myths were invented. All we have a right in this connection to ask is, that the Jew and the unbeliever do not laugh over the Satan and ghost stories and the practice of exorcism reported in the Gospels and Acts, although if those stories were not in those books they would prove more acceptable to intelligent readers now; nor should they deride the quibbling of scholiasts in the theo-philosophical treatises on the Christian dogmas, and the thunderbolts of excommunication which they hurled at one another when they happened to disagree on the details of this matter, although it is exceedingly ridiculous to read it in any history of dogmatics; because the Christian would say to the Jew, You have precisely the same stories in your Talmud, and the same quibbling on these points in your post-Talmudical scholiasts and Kabbalists, who describe heaven and hell, *Gan Eden* and *Gehinnom*, with all that is done, enjoyed and suffered there, with the accuracy and precision with which the schoolboy's text-book describes the surface of the earth. And to the unbeliever the Christian might well say, You do not believe in one devil, but you believe in many. You who make hocus-pocus with the spirits and believe in rapping and tapping, in vulgar soothsaying and witchcraft, in dark arts performed in the dark, you must not laugh over the ghost stories of other people. Again the Jew has the right to say to the Christian, You have no right to laugh over the absurdities and ghost stories of the Talmud and its expounders of the past, when you believe in a personal Satan who tempted and tried the Son of God, absurdity can hardly go beyond this; when you believe the ghost stories and exorcisms of the New Testament, which are certainly glaring enough to defy reason and override all intelligence. The greatest miracles of the Talmud are mere child's play in comparison to the immaculate conception, the resurrection of the crucified one from death and his *post-mortem* feats on earth, in Hades and then in Heaven. So Jew, Christian and Mohammedan might well say to one another, Laugh not at me, look at your own.

We, however, who have no reason to believe absurdities, because they are written in the Talmud or any other book; who adhere to the first principles of reason and the Sinaic revelation, and rely in nowise or manner upon the evidence of miracles; who reject whatever is unnatural in thought, fancy or deed, and adhere steadfastly to the dicta of reason and the Sinaic standard of rectitude, its command of righteousness and holiness, and its demonstration of providence, freedom and immortality, I mean those who are true and upright in these matters, we do not laugh, we do not ridicule, we do not scorn, we understand and appreciate that wonderful things have been written for bearded children, for ignorant multitudes, for masses unable to reason for themselves, and have been written with the best intentions to improve and elevate the human mind, to impress neglected humanity with the sublime truths of God, providence, justice, holiness and immortality, in ages and localities unfit and unable to think in the abstract form, although they were certainly not written for men of advanced intelligence. We can not laugh at those things, we can only see in them the moral and intellectual altitude of certain people for whom those things were written, and attempt to ascertain the intentions of those writers, who are certainly teachers of righteousness and intended the education of mankind. We have a right to say, why do you make so much noise over your salvation if there is no devil and no hell to be saved from? Why do you speak and write so much of that unknown world if you know no more and no better than we do? What means that terror of damnation if you can not form the remotest idea of either damnation or salvation? But if you imagine or believe that you know all that which reason and the Sinaic revelation do not teach, you are welcome to it, if it gives you satisfaction and pleasure; but grant us the privilege at least to imagine and believe that we know those things better, or at least equally as well as you do. We do not laugh at you and you shall not sneer at us. We do not call you superstitious, and you shall not call us stiff-necked and hard-hearted. We do not avoid you, and you shall not pursue us. We do not advise God to exclude any human being from His love and grace, and you shall not arm your God with thunderbolts to crush and condemn us. " I am (for) peace, and when they speak (it is) for war." This verse might also be rendered thus, " I am for peace, although they may be all for war, whenever they speak."

There can be no doubt that neither in reason nor the Sinaic revelation there could be an idea of a hell, a devil, evil spirits or unclean spirits. There is no mention in that revelation of any future reward or punishment in any form, simply because whatever man can not understand can not be revealed to him in words; and man can not and does not understand a state of purely spiritual existence. Therefore wherever men have spoken of that existence they were obliged to express their thoughts and sentiments in concrete and anthropomorphous terms, which may have been correctly understood at the time, but must necessarily sound absurd to posterity, who know not the spiritual idea connected then and there with the concrete and anthropomorphous expression; and the Sinaic revelation was originally intended to be universally and correctly understood. Language has no word now for immortality and must resort to the negative expression of *not mortal;* nor has it a term to express the purely spiritual state of existence. The Jews coined the expression *Hisharath han-Nephesh,* " Preservation of the soul" for immortality, but they found no term by which to denote the state of future existence, because it is as incomprehensible as the quodity of God. We know that God is, and know in part from nature, history and revelation what He does and what he desires man to do; but we know not what and how He is. So we can only know that the soul is an immortal spirit as revelation teaches and reason affirms; but we can not know what and how the soul is in the body or outside thereof, in time or in eternity. It is self-evident, therefore, that we can not understand the nature of the reward or punishment to be administered to the disembodied soul; hence all presentations of a hell, hell-fire, torments, brimstone, large devil and small devils, from the standpoint of reason and the Sinaic revelation, are radically false and purely fictitious. Wherever the term Satan occurs in Scriptures, it must be taken as a fiction, a personification of " hindrance" to do certain things.

The idea of some kind of a reward and punishment after death, the precise nature of which is unknown, is frequently expressed figuratively in the Bible. The sacred writers speak frequently of *Sheol;* and *Sheol* does not signify HELL, for Jacob said of himself, " I will go down mourning to my son (Joseph) to *Sheol.*" (Genesis xxxv. 37.) The term singnifies " netherworld," an abode for the souls of the departed, very deep below (Job xi. 8), where all are alike (*Ibid.* iii. 12 c. s.), all must go there (Isaiah xiv.), the King and his servants, the great and the small, old or young, rich or poor, all go to *Sheol*. No hell-fire, no particular suffering, no diabolic torments are mentioned or even hinted at in connection with the soul's abode in Sheol. It rather appears that all become there *Rephaim*, slumbering and dreaming shades, conscious of their own deeds and unconscious of the outer world, living purely subjective and without connection with any existing object, a sort of dream life, in which a person's consciousness of his wickedness and misdeeds is his punishment, as on the other hand the consciousness of goodness and holiness is his reward. It appears to have been the idea that the soul deprived of its bodily organism could only have subjective existence and recognize only itself and its own doings and omissions without the ability to recognize objects of any kind, which is done by bodily organs.

Not all souls, however, remain forever in that condition. The pious rise from that lower to the higher region, or to a state of higher life, or even to that highest state which is called *Visio Dei essentialis*, " to enjoy the luster of the Shekinah." This hope and belief is frequently expressed by David, Job and other Bible worthies. "Jehovah bringeth up from Sheol my soul, enliveneth me from among those that go down in the pit; sing to Jehovah, all His pious ones, and give thanks to the memorial of His holiness" (Psalms xxx.), saith David, and the sons of Karah repeat the same idea thus: "Elohim only will (or can) redeem my soul from Sheol, when he will take me. Selah." (*Ibid.* xlix. 16.) David said, "Thou abandonest not my soul to Sheol, thou sufferest not thy pious ones to see corruption; thou wilt make known unto me the path of life, the fulness of joys (which are) with thy countenance, the pleasantness (which is) at thy right hand forever" (Psalm xvi.), which is the Biblical foundation for the *Visio Dei essentialis*; and Job in his suffering exclaims that he would cheerfully bear up under the oppressive burden of visitation and wait hopefully in Sheol until the time of his change would come; if he was sure that God would find him worthy of that higher state of life after death. (Job xiv. 13-14.) For another sacred bard had said, probably before Job, "Not the dead will praise God, and not all of those who go down to silence (to Sheol); but we (the " blessed ones of Jevovah "—verse 15) will praise the Lord from now and forever, Hallelujah." (Psalms cxv. 15-18.) The Prophet Isaiah expressed the hope, *Ve'eretz Rephaim thappil*, "The land of the shades (Sheol) thou wilt cause to fall"; to which he added, *Billa ham-Maveth lan-Netzach*, "Death will be swallowed in eternity, and Jehovah will wipe the tear from every countenance." (Isaiah xxv. 8.) He evidently believed that there is also in Sheol a progress from lower to higher conditions for all human beings; or that the progress of man on earth to higher and clearer self-consciousness by the universal triumphs of enlightenment and holiness will deprive Sheol of its inhabitants, in consequence of the solidarity of the human family. This is the Biblical foundation of eschatology without devil, hell, brimstone or any particular instruments of torture and any offense to human reason.

We have to add to this the conservation, constancy and universality of force, viz: that the same forces remain and are equally efficient at all times and in all parts of the universe. Call the sentient and intelligent soul a force, and you do at once understand its immortality. The Sinaic revelation is the proof for the immortal and God-like nature of man; and the principle of justice, which includes the ideas of reward and punishment. The law of God-like force is to outlast time and be the same in eternity; hence there must be reward and punishment also hereafter. In as far, however, as moral wrongs are subjective only, and its consequences are limited in time, so must the punishment be subjective and limited in time. In as far as the good and true is eternal, so must be its reward. The righteous and self-conscious souls arise to that glory which we can not understand in this state of existence; the wicked and brutal men who never rose to a state of pure self-consciousness in this life, punish themselves in Sheol, until God in his mercy shall call them from subjective stupor to objective cogitation, which we again understand not. This is. Bible eschatology without any interference with God or human reason, and without any means of salvation besides righteousness, holiness rationality freedom and progress.

GIFTS OF GRACE, REDEMPTION AND SALVATION.
PART I.

An ancient prophet said (Micah vi. 6): "Wherewith shall I approach *Jehovah*, bow myself before the High *Elohim?* Shall I approach Him with burnt offerings, with calves of a year old? Can *Jehovah* be pleased with thousands of rams, or with ten thousand rivers of oil? Shall I give my first-born for my transgression, the fruit of my body for the sin of my soul? He hath told thee, O! man, what is good, and what *Jehovah*, thy *Elohim*, requireth of thee; it is but to do justice, to love goodness, and to walk unostentatiously with thy *Elohim*." This simple passage contains the old, old questions of the religious mind, viz, wherewith shall the mortal being appear before the Majesty on High, the Lord of the universe, or which are the proper means of worship? Are the fat rams of Bashan or the streams of oil acceptable to Him? And the next question is, how shall the poor sinner atone for his transgressions before Him who is most pure and most holy? Shall I give the best and dearest I have as a ransom for my guilty soul; which are the means of redemption, redemption from the yoke of sin and guilt? How shall I purify and elevate my soul to save it from the pangs of guilt and the domain of death, to rest in peace in *Sheol*, and be entitled to the hope that the Almighty will call me from the dream-life of *Sheol* to the fulness of joy which is in His presence, the pleasantness and bliss which are at His right hand forever? Which are the means of salvation? They must be in man and not outside of him, as the capacities of sin and self-destruction are also in him. They must be in human will and reason as the ability to soar aloft is in the bird. So, it appears, that prophet thought who, in answering those momentous questions, points out means within the power of the human will and the counsel of the individual reason; be right, be good, be true and be saved, so, O! man, thou hast been told, the prophet advises. Be redeemed by righteousness, be saved by the love of the good and the true; by opening widely the portals of reason for the King of Glory to come in; by expanding the soul and unfolding its capacities, to rise above the chains of matter, the prison of the demi-conscious dream-life and the self-delusion of passion's powerless slave; to rise to the throne of glory. This is resurrection in fact, rising in this life from *Sheol* to the throne of glory, "the nearness of God"; and for all we know, it is also in life hereafter the rising of the soul from *Sheol* to the "nearness of

God," by the inherent abilities to rise from dim consciousness and self-deceit to the sunny height of glory and joy, in a state of clear and full self-consciousness.

This appears to be the idea of that prophet and of all prophets who received their inspiration from Mount Sinai. But it appears to be too simple to be true and too natural to be satisfactory in the estimation of dogmatic theologians. "For God hath made man right, and they seek many reckonings." Ever since man has reached the consciousness of his superiority to the brute, he has asked the same identical questions in the most different forms: Which are the proper means of worship, of atonement, of redemption, of salvation? And the answers are almost as numerous as the stars and, in the majority of cases, as absurd and illogical as the madman's dance. It is hard to say what folly and cruelty man has not committed under the impression that he would thus please and appease the gods and save his soul from perdition. From the human victims sacrificed to Pagan gods to the *autos-da-fe* of civilized barbarians; from the self-destruction of the infatuated Hindoo seeking atonement for his sins to the Flagelants, hermits, ascetics, monks and nuns for the greater glory of God, reaching down to our very doors; from the dancing, fighting, wounding priests of Baal on Mount Carmel, and the women weeping and lamenting over the descent of Thammuz or Adonis to the nether world down to the shouting, dancing, shaking and screaming fraternities of our days; from the unchaste women in the Heathen temples and the crazed ones howling and leaping for the glory of Cerus and Bacchus; from the wars of extermination, with all their terrors, waged in behalf of this or that god, this or that dogma, waged by nation against nation, sect against sect, or priest against priest, down to the milder though no less inhuman form of persecution and exclusion for opinion's sake; from animal victims slaughtered upon the altar on Mount Moriah to victimized reason sacrificed in seminaries and churches; from the Jew's and Musselman's circumcision to the Christian sacrament of baptism; from the Jew's and Musselman's fasts to cancel their sins to the Christian's eating and drinking the transubstantiated flesh and blood of the Savior for the very same end, with all the mysteries and absurdities connected with the rites; it is safe to maintain that there is hardly an absurdity, a folly or cruelty invented by imagination which at one time or another has not been used as a holy rite, and conscientiously practiced in this or that corner of the earth as means of worshiping God, atoning for sins, obtaining redemption and achieving salvation.

Most remarkable, perhaps, in this matter is, that people with these facts before their eyes, can not convince themselves that means and forms are subject to change, hence that none of them could be intended to be everlasting, to suit all men under all climates and under all circumstances; furthermore that all means and forms, observances and practices, whatever end they may have in view, if they are foolish or absurd, *i. e.*, contrary to reason, barbarous or cruel, *i. e.*, contrary to humanitarian principles, or even unæsthetic and offensive to the refined taste of any age or locality, they must also be contrary to the Law of God, for the end does not justify any bad means. And yet, in those very means and forms, observances and practices, there is the main cause of the " Disagreements " among Jews, Christians and Mohammedans. As nearly as men can agree on abstract questions, all agree on the main principles of faith, the principal doctrines of religion; all stand upon the platform of the Sinaic revelation, and all intend and hope to enter the everlasting covenant between God and man. The " Disagreements " reduce themselves exclusively to means and forms.

The worst in this matter is, that those very " Disagreements " were and are even now, to a certain extent, the causes of bewildering superstitions and ridiculous prejudices of man against his neighbor, which clog reason and obscure the conscience; and of that wild and reckless fanaticism which is fraught with nameless misery and woe. Because it is so, one should think it is the duty of every philanthropist to wage war upon all those means and forms, observances and practices, which cause the mischief, the separation, disintegration and hostility. But unfortunately man can not do without them; history proves that he can not. Man can not be and will never be without religion, and religion consists of abstract truths, doctrines, precepts and commandments, which are essentially spiritual and formally abstract. These abstract truths must be reduced to practice by tangible means, concrete forms, inherited observances, which become holier by age and important by general consent. Besides there are quite a number of people who never reason, never reflect, never think beyond a certain limit. With them the concrete form has assumed the importance of the spirit. You break the form, and all their religion with its hope and consolation, with its soothing, controlling and guiding effects, is lost to them. You say they worship the form or the means, they are idolators, let their idolatry be destroyed for the sake of truth. Perhaps they are; but they are nevertheless men and brethren and fellow-creatures and children of your God and mine, you must take care of them, you dare not deprive them of that religion which they possess, which satisfies, controls and guides them. Therefore, the philanthropist must be slow and considerate in his attempts to eradicate those causes of evils which befall man.

On the other hand those means and forms are of grave importance to the most intelligent as well as to the most illiterate. However intelligent, learned and enlightened a man may be, he must nevertheless tell himself, I do believe in God, revelation, providence, freedom, justice, the brotherhood and immortality of man; I do not wish to tear these convictions out of my soul, and even if I should, I could not do it, for I can not change human nature, nor can I control the power of reason and conscience whose dicta these beliefs are. I must naturally ask myself: How shall I express the veneration, gratitude and love which I feel to my Maker; how shall I worship Him, for whom my soul yearns and pants, as panteth the hart after the brooks of water? and how shall I give utterance to the regret, the sorrow, the repentance and the remorse I feel over the misdeeds I have committed; how shall I heal the burning wound in my conscience? and how shall I withstand all the temptations of lust and passion, and nourish my soul with goodness and wisdom to escape death and become worthy of God's grace? These are exactly the same questions which the Prophet Micah asked and which every conscientious man must ask himself sometimes. Levity and carelessness in those things may do for awhile, but not forever. Every man has his conscientious scruples; in every man the voice of his better nature speaks at one time or another. The literature of the civilized world suggests that man rather thinks too much than too little over those questions. Four-fifths of the whole Jewish literature, Bible, Talmud and *Midrash* included, treats on these very questions; and the theological library of Christians and Mohammedans is immense.

As man is generally expected to believe too much, which has caused many to believe little or nothing, so is he also expected to do too much for his salvation. The simple answer of the Prophet Micah to those paramount queries. " Be right, be good, be true," was overlooked and submerged under a flood of speculations, in which all those sandbanks and rocks of "Disagreements" threaten destruction to the frail bark of religion. We must look to our chart and compass, to reason and conscience on the one hand, to the Sinaic revelation on the other, in order to ascertain our course, to decide whether the Prophet Micah or the vulgar theology furnishes correct answers to man's paramount queries. Reason answers, man is a complete individual in his physical organism. He is in possession of all those organs and qualities which are necessary to sustain himself and preserve his race. Spiritually also he must be a complete " little world " with all the capacities and faculties to sustain himself and preserve his identity intact as a spiritual individual in time and eternity. As he possesses organs of digestion, nutrition and assimilation, which perform their task without any aid from abroad, so he possesses by the grace of his Maker the capacities and faculties to become free, intelligent, noble, generous, eminently self-conscious, immortal and happy. As he possesses the capacities to reach human perfection, he must be able to reach happiness, for happiness is in perfection only. In as far then as he has reached human perfection, he has reached happiness; and inasmuch as the happiness of perfection is not an organic sensation, it is a spiritual satisfaction, which must be co-eternal with the spirit itself. This is reason's answer to those paramount queries, sealed and confirmed by man's conscience and consciousness. It tells us, man is his own guide and compass. He is the sole author of his own weal or woe. He is his own Heaven or hell. Healthy food and exercise strengthen the body. Healthy moral and spiritual food strengthen the soul. The body grows, so does the soul. The body develops to human perfection, so does the soul, by the nutriment which either of them receives; with the only distinction that the growth of body has its natural limits, as all matter has, and the growth of spirit is subject to no perceptible limits, it is unlimited, and therefore immortal, eternal. It is the will in man, as Elihu said in the Book of Job, which makes of the one a sound, strong and skilled laborer, and of the other a delicate and indolent spectator. It is the will which makes of the one an energetic, intelligent, enlightened, honest and upright apostle of righteousness; and of the other a useless camp-follower. It is the will which rouses one to the height of self-consciousness and immortality and eternal happiness, and leaves the other in a perpetual dream-life here, hence also in *Sheol.* The will and you yourselves are identical. Your will is yourself. It is nothing outside of your own being. You will it earnestly and energetically, and yours must be immortality and happiness; you will it not and remain slumbering in the embrace of vegetable and animal functions here and in *Sheol* there. The will receives incentive and impetus from abroad, you say; but they must go through his reason and conscience, and with the well-developed mind, the well-balanced mind, the will is guided by them, that is to say, the will is free. Will, reason and conscience are no three things, they are the functions of the same soul. In the mind symmetrically developed, reason decides correctly, in perfect consonance with the conscience; and directs the will, as the compass directs the ship. To rise to self-conscious immortality and happiness is in man's power exclusively; it depends on no circumstances and no outer influences. Man is to all intents and purposes a free and independent being. This is the answer of reason to our momentous questions, decisive to all who believe in God and man's God-like nature. The gifts of grace are all in man and in all men.

Does the Sinaic revelation teach the same doctrine? We think it does. Revelation and reason must not contradict each other. Still we can not answer this query until we shall have examined into the means of salvation.

The first means of salvation, they say, is faith. But faith is too indefinite and homonymous a term; none can fix its meaning exactly. It meant one thing with Paul and another with the Church of history, one thing with St. Augustine and another with Albertus Magnus, one thing with the Catholic and another with the Protestant Church, while in its dogmatic sense it has no meaning for the non-Christian. The first means of salvation, known to all and understood by all, is the desire of man to worship God. This desire or volition has its origin in two facts of the consciousness, viz: the consciousness of God as the Supreme Being, on whose power, wisdom and goodness we depend, and whose greatness and glory we admire; and *secondly* the consciousness of man's spiritual and God-like nature, his revelation and accountability to God, his admiration and veneration of the loftiest ideal of the good and the true. This desire or volition to worship God is the ground form of religion. It is not the inactive faith, belief or confidence in the Supreme Being, nor is it a mere emotion or effect produced by external agency. It is a free-will motion of the soul seeking communion with God, rising, as it were, above this world's fluctuations, above its own earthly habitation to the world of spirit and eternity. This desire or volition to worship, so common to man, is the impetus, the incentive to the soul to seek spiritual food in the domain of spirit, to develop, to grow, to proceed and progress on the path toward human perfection and happiness. To this end and purpose, to speak teleologically, this desire was impressed on human nature. One might say, if you wish to ascertain how far you have advanced to immortality and happiness, measure your desire or volition to worship God, and you have the solution of the problem.

Does the Sinaic revelation maintain that this holy desire of man comes from an agency outside of himself? Does it prescribe the methods and forms in which a man should worship God? It does neither, although it begins with the solemn and impressive lesson teaching the One Eternal God and Providence, and by its very fact of God communicating with man impresses one forcibly and indelibly with man's God-like nature. It simply prohibits the having or making of gods, or believing in any besides Jehovah, and commands not to show them that honor which is due only to the GREAT I AM. These honors are expressed in two simple terms, the first of which is subjective, *Lo Thishtachaveh*, personal service or worship; and the second is objective, *Lo Tho'obdem*, worship by objective deeds. So we know that in the Sinaic revelation Israel was commanded to worship God subjectively and objectively, with the inner emotions and motions of man, and with outward deeds. Both points are expounded in Deuteronomy vi. 5, in the *Shema*. Concerning the subjective point it is ordained, "And thou shalt love Jehovah thy Elohim with all thy heart, with all thy soul, and all thy might"; and concerning the objective point, it is commanded that man should perpetually have the laws of God upon his heart, impress them on his children, speak freely and clearly of them, and make them known to his fellow-man by all lawful means of impressing them. That is all the form of worship contained in the Sinaic revelation, to which was added the permission to erect an altar of earth, simple and transitory, because the whole civilized world then worshiped by sacrifices, which was a mere permission without the intention of permanency.

When Moses constructed a state with its policy and polity upon the Sinaic principles with special reference to the wants and habits of his people then and there, he organized for them a sacrificial culte with a special priesthood, similar to what they had seen and venerated in Egypt; although in ordaining those laws he certainly could not think of permanency, as none could prescribe for all coming generations how to worship. Forms and methods change; eternal in these laws is only the Sinaic command, that man should worship God both subjectively and objectively, in himself and by good deeds outside of himself. Therefore the methods and forms of divine worship changed so often in Israel and among all denominations believing in the Sinaic revelation. The principle, however, remained that worship must be intelligent, humane and spiritual, within the soul and by its own promptings and the manifestation of good, noble and generous deeds; to Jehovah only and none besides Him.

Here is one of the means of grace, its name is divine worship, free, noble, intelligent and humane. The Sinaic revelation acknowledges this as the first means of grace, to rouse the soul to human perfection, to immortality and the happiness of perfection. In this point, you see, the Sinaic revelation fully corresponds with the dicta of reason. There is no hostility and no conflict between reason and revelation. The gifts of grace are in man, and his is the freedom and ability to make proper use of them.

I am sorry that I can not finish my subject this evening, and beg you to hear me again on this subject next Friday evening.

XV.
GIFTS OF GRACE, REDEMPTION AND SALVATION.
PART II.

The innate desire of man to worship is a gift of grace bestowed upon him by his Maker. It is in him, part and parcel of his very nature. It remains with him from the early dawn of consciousness to the hour of death. It rouses him to seek that which is higher and holier than carnal pleasures, to long for the eternal and absolute, and prompts him to yearn after spiritual nutriment, on which the soul grows, thrives, develops and rises to human perfection and happiness, immortality and bliss. It is the most efficient gift of grace. As soon as one begins to think correctly of God, his own soul, and the relation of both, he becomes a better man; inasmuch as he rises above the vulgar venality and sensuality of his animal nature, steps, so to say, outside of himself, and seeks an ideal of perfection above himself. When this fundamental knowledge moves his will to that intense volition to worship, to admire, to venerate and to adore that highest ideal of perfection, he has become wide awake to the destiny of man, to develop and train himself to an immortal being, a pure and self-conscious personality. He is on his way to salvation. The desire to worship is the first gift of grace, the innate means to rise from earth to heaven, from darkness to light, from brutal selfishness to human perfection, from *Sheol* to the presence of the Most High. It is the only form of resurrection of which we can form a distinct idea. Man rises from his cosmic existence to the dignity of a spiritual personality, as the planet emerges from the boundless sea of cosmic matter to the condition of an individual body.

The struggle between sensuality and spirituality, selfishness and universality, darkness and light, death and immortality, is in the nature of man. He could not be man without it; he would be either brute or angel. He could not have a free will, hence his virtues and vices would be equally indifferent. We can not tell why it is so, but we know that it is so; nor do we know about any existence why it is so, we can only know that it is so. The moral law is based upon that existent struggle. The education of man is accomplished under it. His goodness is the sum total of victories in this perpetual combat. His wickedness is made up of the defeats which he sustained. No man is without his victories, none without his defeats in this process of life, the dialectics of antitheses, the continual culmination of heterogeneous elements. The sinless man is a fantasm, a theological fiction, like the mathematical point and the atom in science, a thought-thing without reality. Dogmatics fancied a sinless man, who, as a legitimate sequence, had to be made a god; for a sinless man is something like a mountain without a valley, which is simply unthinkable.

In this struggle between good and evil, in which man is engaged to the very moment of his death, he is given a natural ally which is another gift of grace; its name is repentance. Like the desire of worship the feeling of repentance is specifically human, not a trace of which is discernible in the individuals of the two organic kingdoms. Man, he often knows not why, repents his misdeeds, and he does so by his own free will, by peculiar emotions of his conscience. Instinctively he feels dissatisfied, a feeling of shame comes over him, which is followed by remorse and not seldom by self-contempt and the ardent wish not to have committed that misdeed. First he suspects that every man knows of his wickedness, so that the slightest allusion to it, or even an accidental word, irritates and mortifies him; until it dawns in his soul that the all-seeing eye of God beholds the deeds of man and nothing is hidden before it. Then awakens in him that burning pain which has driven so many to despair, madness and self-destruction; that undeniable hell-fire, which consumes the marrow of life and burneth to the lowest *Sheol*. It follows him on the path of life like an evil demon, it retires with him to his solitary chamber, troubles him in his dreams, and rises with him from his couch to torment him again.

Repentance, this most humiliating and most aggravating of all feelings, rises in man; it comes not from without; rises from the free will and the consciousness of the good in man, to war upon his own wickedness, his own misdeeds; to burn them out of his soul; to turn him away from the path of evil; to prompt him to seek a higher standard of rectitude and a firmer will to be guided by it; and wherever it may be possible to repair the mischief done and obliterate the cause and effect of sin. It is the gift of grace given alike to Jew and Christian, Mohammedan and Pagan. It is roused in man by a number of causes, many of which are seemingly accidental; but it is chiefly aroused in him by the exercise of the first gift of grace, viz: the desire to worship. He places himself before God; he stands before the All-just; he compares himself with the Most High; he attempts to commune and to converse with the Most Holy; he must necessarily become aware of his own faults and shortcomings, and behold the writing on the wall, *Menai, Menai, Thekel, Upharsin*. It is this natural association of ideas, and not either circumcision or baptism, either a particular act of grace or the function of a holy ghost or a personal *Yetzer hattob*; either this or that particular form of worship which rouses in man this second gift of grace, repentance, from potentiality to actuality. In this connection it certainly depends not upon how he worships, it depends upon what he worships. The form is indifferent. If one worships the Most Holy God, the God of justice and truth, the Eternal God of the Sinaic revelation whose insignia are truth, justice and purity, worship must lead him to repentance of sin, with or without sacrifices, fasts or sacraments.

Few men will deny that the consciousness of guilt and crime with its shame, remorse, self-contempt, genuine and sincere repentance is the only knowable hell-fire. The doubts begin with the question, Does repentance work atonement? or, in other words, does God forgive sins because the sinner repents? This is a point of "Disagreement" among the various denominations. The ancient teachers of Judaism maintained *En l'cho Dabar she-omed mippenei hat-Theshuba*. " Nothing (no sin) can stand before repentance." Repentance wipes out every guilt, it burns out every sin. It is the baptism with fire. They prescribed various means to assist the efficacy of repentance, like confession, humiliation before God and man (no auricular confession), prayer, fasting and abstinence in general, the giving of alms, and practicing other humanitarian benevolence, exercising the mind in the study of God's law, and such other means; but they are the means only to express and actualize the change of mind and to strengthen the will of the sinner, in walking steadfastly on the path of righteousness, and are of no avail without the main gift of grace, viz: sincere and genuine repentance of misdeeds and the thorough change of mind. They learned this of the ancient Prophets of Israel, who knew of no other means to obliterate sin besides repentance and change of mind. Neither sacrifices nor fasts, neither afflictions nor prayers were looked upon by them as means of atonement. In all forms of speech they called men to repentance, and promised in the most beautiful metaphors remission of sins to the repenting sinner. Those ancient teachers and prophets understood the Laws of Moses to the effect that the sacrifices and the observances connected therewith were mere symbols, simple means in correspondence with that age and its tastes, to express and actualize the change of mind, to strengthen and satisfy the morbid will of the sinner. Sin is subjective; God is not offended; man is lowered and disgraced by it. Repentance is self-punishment and self-elevation. It purges the soul and starts it on its upward way to God and righteousness. In so far as sin is objective in its effects upon our fellow-men, it is the penitent's duty to repair the breach, to amend the damage and appease the injured fellow-man. The penitent must obliterate both the cause and the effect of his sins. The penitent punishes and corrects himself. If he succeeds therein every other punishment or correction would be unjust and unnecessary, and must not be expected of the All-just

God, of whom we are told : " The Rock, perfect are His doings, for all his ways are justice, a God of faithfulness and no wrong, righteous and upright is He."

Mohammedanism, in the main, adopted this Jewish idea of remission of sins by repentance, although it proposes other means in addition to those of the Jewish prophets and rabbis. In the New Testament both John and Jesus announce the coming of the Kingdom of Heaven by repentance. The idea of vicarious atonement is the product of the Christianity of history, not of its founder or founders, as I believe I have proved in my little book, " The Martyrdom of Jesus of Nazareth," and I do not like to repeat my own arguments. This *ex-post facto* speculation forms the main body of Christian dogmatics, and is based upon the hypothesis that the death of the Messiah must have been a special act of Providence for some specific purpose. Gradually the expounders persuaded themselves into the belief that he died as a sacrifice of atonement for the sins of others. The idea suggested itself from an ancient belief of Semitic Pagans, like the King of Moab, who sacrificed the sons of kings to obviate national calamities, and was utilized to convert Heathen and also Jews, after the altar had been destroyed, the ancient polity abrogated, and they were left without their time-honored form of worship. It belongs to the class of means; it is not principle, and is without the least foundation in Moses, the Prophets, the Rabbis, Jesus and even Paul. The Sinaic revelation informs us that only one sin, viz : taking the name of God in vain, is so grievous that God would not hold him guiltless who commits it. This, of course, suggests that other sins are forgiven, as it is plainly stated in the supplementary revelation, " He forgiveth iniquity, transgression and sin." But the idea of vicarious atonement has no foothold in that revelation. Therefore, the Christian theologians adopted the whole Jewish theory of the remission of sins, and added the vicarious atonement, which appears superfluous to Jews and Mohammedans. Moses informs us that God said to him, when he offered himself as a vicarious atonement, " Him, who sinned unto me, will I blot out from my book." The Prophet Ezekiel said, " The person that sinneth, he shall be put to death." Justice dictates that the guilty one be punished, and not the innocent instead of the guilty. Reason responds, if the effect of sin is in me, a stain in my soul, it can no more be removed by the meritorious deeds of another person than I could be cured of any disease by the remedy which my physician swallows. If sin is a negative quantity, that I have so much less spiritual substance in my soul as I have neglected my duties to God and man, neglected to increase and grow in goodness and enlightenment; then all the surplus which others might possess, can as little replace the deficiency in me as the years of his life could be added to mine, or mine to his, to make up any relative deficiency. If the solidarity of mankind goes so far that all mankind has but one soul, as some Christian theologians advanced, and God or his Son died for the sin of that all-soul; then the individual can not commit sin, and needs no atonement, and the death of the Son is the atonement for all, Heathens, cannibals, murderers, Jews and infidels included, and whatever we poor mortals do is perfectly indifferent, as the all-soul or the soul of all is redeemed anyhow. We can find no reason for the doctrine of vicarious atonement, either Scriptural or philosophical, and we have no need of any hypothesis, doctrine or dogma to explain the life and death, the work and offices of the Messiah, his godhead or manhood, his resurrection or second advent, as we who stand upon the standpoint of the Sinaic revelation and reason need no Messiah whatever, and no Messianic doctrines in any form, as I believe I have proved in my last course of lectures " On the Origin and History of the Messianic Idea." We propose to believe as much as we rationally can, and no more. When we are asked to believe and to do more than is necessary, more than is reasonable, we must beg to be excused.

You see we all agree in principle, viz, that sins are forgiven. We also agree that there could be no remission of sins without sincere and genuine repentance. We furthermore agree in most of the means, such as humiliation before God and man, confession, giving alms and the like. But we disagree in other means, and the dogma of vicarious atonement is no more than that. From this one " Disagreement " many others arise, so many, indeed, that they divide the believers in the Sinaic revelation into three main religious bodies and numerous·small factions or sects. This makes of Christianity a tribal and sectional religion in conflict with man's reason. Therefore, those who believe in the universal and eternal character of the Sinaic revelation and the final triumph of God's truth can hardly doubt that this " Disagreement " also will be overcome, and the religion of the future man will contain no Christology. The future man will need no Messiah and no redeemer, no baptism and no circumcision, no months, no weeks, no days of fasting and atonement, and no sacraments of bread and wine, no mediator in Heaven and none on earth, no priest and no rites, in order to secure salvation for his soul; for neither of all these and all other means are contained in the Sinaic revelation or based upon the pure dicta of reason. Whatever is not either in revelation or reason is of the spontaneous generation of fancy and purely accidental. Fantasms and accidental productions last as long as they are serviceable to man, so long and no longer, the true only is eternal, and this must be found either in reason or revelation. The future man, if our means of preservation and communication be not miraculously destroyed, will see the noonday of enlightenment, discard all superstitions and recognize means as mere means, forms of a transitory nature; then " Agreement " will grow out of " Disagreement," and I venture to say the following articles of faith will satisfy the most pious souls:

1. I believe in One, Eternal and Universal Jehovah.
2. I believe in man's godlike nature, with capacities to become free, just, pure, true, immortal and happy.
3. I believe in God's Law contained in the Sinaic revelation as the standard of rectitude, the path of righteousness, the proof of God's providence and man's immortality by his godlike nature.
4. I believe in man's desire to worship God and the free will repentance in his own conscience as the gifts of grace, to lead man onward to God on the path of righteousness and upward to Him, immortality, human perfection and the happiness of perfection.
5. I believe in the freedom and equality of all men as the law of God and the final and universal triumph of reason, justice and goodness over all obstacles.

These five articles of faith, I opine, will satisfy them, to which I only would wish to add, I believe that ignorance is the original sin and stupidity is universal depravity, which must be vanquished by free schools, free press, free speech and free thought.

I believe what all good and great men have said and thought in their respective times and places, provided I be permitted to be my own judge as to what is good, useful, practicable and applicable also in my time and place.

This would complete the holy number seven, to which nothing ought to be added; or else I would propose this No. 8: I believe all that is necessary for man to believe, provided it is not in antagonism with reason and conscience and the Sinaic revelation.

I do not mean to say that you should believe this and no more, or that I do, for man is in many respects the product of history. No man can successfully deny his parents and their teachings, although he is in nowise exactly like them. Every generation varies and progresses. Gradually only opinions, like types, change. But as both change and progress after all, the religion of the future man, whenever that may be, might be based upon those articles of faith. It is evident that we are advancing to some such ultimate point as the universal republic, universal religion, one God and one human family. If the world is satisfied to reach that objective point at once, we Jews are satisfied and willing to join the mutual benevolent society of all mankind, with the firm conviction that this is the will of God and the ultimate destiny of man on earth.

XVI.

THE JUDAISM OF HISTORY.

Man, they maintain, is the creature of circumstances. This is true of minors whose understanding is not strong enough to resist the outer influences and to govern them, and of that class of childlike people who never reach the estate of maturity and personal independence. The accomplished man rises above the circumstances and governs them. According to the philosophy of Moses Maimonides on Providence, the accomplished man, *i. e.*, the intelligent and righteous, is governed by his reason, by means of which, and in proportion to his perfection, Providence is manifested in him and counsels him; while the neglected man, *i. e.*, the thoughtless and wicked, is the play-ball of accident and casualty to the same extent as the other individuals of the animal and vegetable kingdoms. Man is no more the result of his parents than the candle light is the result of the gas flame at which it was lit, or *vice versa*. He inherits dispositions, and no more than that; and all dispositions are subject to reason and conscience. Like Isaac and Rebecca, many parents have two sons, or even twin-brothers, the one of which becomes Israel, " the prince of the Lord," and the other an Esau, a rough hunter.

The forms and methods, however, which are the instruments and implements of reason and conscience to become actualized and influential, are of slow growth. They are constructed and crystalized by experience and repeated application, hence they are inherited from generation to generation. Reason and conscience submit to them only by the force of authority, the authority of parents and teachers, political and church government, tradition and literature. Forms and methods are inherited, imposed like the different styles of garments. Therefore, we can speak of a Judaism, Christianity or Mohammedanism of history, as these religious systems developed their peculiar forms and methods in course of time, although all three of them started from the Sinaic revelation; without admitting for a moment that reason and conscience are not the superior authority, to which to appeal our right is reserved; or that the "Differences" in those three religious systems are not the mere disagreements in form and method.

Let us review first the Judaism of history. According to the testimony of the Pentateuch, Moses was the first teacher of forms and methods, to actualize the Sinaic principles, doctrines and laws for the practical life of a nation. He built up a State upon the underlying principles of the moral law with its two pillars of freedom and equality; and a religion with its polity upon the basis of pure monotheism, the most high and most holy One in covenant with Israel. Like all eminent statesmen and legislators, he was obliged to do justice to inherited forms, methods and institutions, and subordinated them to the system on which he built. While in the construction of the State and the laws, he was obliged to accept slavery, bigamy, the avenger of blood, the law of retaliation, the right of conquest and other heritages; he modified them according to the underlying principle, abolishing slavery among the Hebrews and protecting the heathen slave by humane enactments; establishing the freedom and equal rights of woman, to counteract polygamy, and ordaining monogamy for the priest as a pattern to the people; the cities of refuge to counteract the barbarity of bloody revenge; the ransom with money in the case of bodily injuries, to modify the law of retaliation; the system of voluntary military service exclusively, with laws to protect the lives of non-combatants, property and female chastity, in case of war to counteract wars of conquest, and so on. There was so much barbarism to be obliterated that he could not overcome all of it at once. He did the same thing precisely in the religious institutions. He could not eradicate the ancient and universal form of worship by bloody sacrifices, and could only regulate and modify it in accordance with the underlying Sinaic principles. He gave them a harmless priesthood, which was a mere shadow of the mighty priesthood of Egypt. At the same time he taught them two other forms of worship, one in the practice of charity and benevolence, and another in maintaining and preserving the Law, the rights, claims, liberties, intelligence, morality, happiness and well-being of God's chosen people, the perpetuation of the divine covenant. He taught them that the objective form of divine worship consists not of the sacrifices only; charity and benevolence, justice and righteousness, the protection of freedom and the advancement of enlightenment are other forms of divine worship no less acceptable to the most high and most holy God than any other form.

The Israelites obeyed or rebelled, went through periods of national glory and happiness or degradation and misery. The logical and illogical elements, the Sinaic revelation and the world's Paganism, the civilizing and enlightening agency of the laws of Moses and the barbarism of the surrounding nations, light and darkness collided in the course of history, so that the one now and the other then was victorious in Israel. When idolatry and despotism domineered on the one side, and on the other the sacrificial *culte* degenerated into another form of Paganism, the Prophets arose and thundered those divine messages into the ears of the deluded masses, corrupt priests and kings, called them back home to the Sinaic revelation, the divine covenant, the wise and benevolent laws of Moses, and Judaism became in their hand a purely spiritual religion, as its essence is, without any particular forms besides those advanced by Moses to counterpoise the sacrificial polity. Besides Ezekiel, who proposed reforms in the institutions of public worship, which, however, were never adopted, the Prophets advocated no kind of forms and methods, so that Judaism became purely spiritual in their hands. Therefore, they succeeded only in improving the morals, enlightening the minds, correcting abuses, diminishing the importance attached to forms, and directing the minds to the essence and import of the Law; and could not change practically anything either in the form of government or in the inherited forms and methods in general. The progress achieved was in the spreading spirituality and the clearer conceptions of the religious and moral truths among the accessible portion of the people, and stirring up that national self-consciousness which saved the nation from utter amalgamation with the surrounding nationalities, and then among those of Assyria and Babylonia.

[Permit me to remark here that the peculiar hypothesis of modern critics who set Moses after the Prophets is historically illegitimate and philosophically untenable; because there is no cause to assume that the writers of the sacred history did not know better than their critics of from two thousand to three thousand years later; no cause to assume that the authors of the holiest books of mankind were willful impostors; no cause to assume that the loftiest and purely spiritual aspect of any religion or code of laws preceded its concrete, practical and popular state.]

After fifty years of captivity in Babylon, forty two thousand men, with their families, returned to Palestine to re-establish the Hebrew people upon its ancient soil. The first public act of theirs was to rebuild the altar and then the temple, and revive the ancient form of worship, precisely as it was before. They would not and could not change the form, although besides the law of the covenant, the doctrine and laws of the Sinaic revelation, they made no attempt to introduce again the Mosaic law. Seventy years later, when Ezra and then Nehemiah came to Palestine, the laws of Moses considerably modified were reintroduced, together, however, with new enactments and methods. It was a new phase of Judaism, which was again considerably modified by the advance of Grecian culture into Asia, from and after the time of Alexander the Great. Persian, and afterward Grecian elements, amalgamated with purely Jewish. The Scribes gradually took the place of the priests and prophets. They expounded the Law and also the Prophets, thus expounded and translated, it was no longer the living original. The additions and changes in the temple service were numerous and characteristic. The synagogues replaced the altars upon the " Heights," the Thorah replaced the Ark of the Covenant, prayers, hymns and music, teaching and expounding assumed the importance of sacrifices and priestly rites, and gradually a new phase of Judaism took root among the people.

The attempt at a sudden and abrupt change of forms and methods by Grecized Hebrews and Antiochus Epiphanes with his lieutenants, led to the remarkable rebellion under the Maccabees and resulted in a complete victory of the orthodox element and the independence of the country. But the natural and gradual change of forms and methods remained the very same as before, and went on without restriction. New laws were made, new customs established, new methods were invented to expound the ancient laws, new forms took the place of the older, and new parties, Pharisees, Sadducees and Essenes, stepped in with new issues. When finally the Hebrew commonwealth was overthrown, the capital, temple and altar were destroyed, the ancient polity was abrogated, the casement was broken, and the new form and method of Judaism, gradually developed during previous centuries, at once took the place of the older forms and methods which had been dropped or changed gradually, imperceptibly and naturally. It appeared as rabbinical Judaism on the one hand, and as Messianic or denationalized Judaism, afterward Christianity, on the other hand. The literatures on both sides are the *Mishnah, Tosephta. Mechilta, Saphra, Siphri* and some minor books on the part of the Jews, and the New Testament on the part of the Messiahists. Both literatures were committed to writing nearly simultaneously, in the second century of the Christian Era. That Jewish literature mentioned contains the forms and methods, the laws, customs, doctrines and peculiar opinions of that new phase of Judaism together with the history of that evolution and reconstruction, and many reminiscences and episodes scientific, historical, homiletical and juridical. That literature cast the new phase of Judaism into a stereotyped form, just as the New Testament was the stereotyped form for the other side, from which gradually rose the Christianity of history. The principal work done by the rabbis or *Tana'im* of the first and second centuries was to collect, compile, criticise and systematize the material left from the Second Commonwealth of the Hebrews. This material, however, was but partly written and in a variety of scrolls. Much of it was verbally preserved and communicated traditionally, and consisted in part of customs, maxims and precepts not found directly in the Bible. It was believed, however that " The custom of Israel is law," hence every existing custom, maxim or precept must have its root in the laws of Moses. Special methods of expounding the law, the Rabbinical Hermeneutics, were established not only in order to preserve every iota of that heritage, but also to prove that it is all founded upon the Bible. This apparatus of the *Tana'im* is a portion of the rabbinical literature just mentioned.

The teachers then certainly supposed that their labors had established and finished the new phase of Judaism. They may have overlooked that the very material which they compiled, systematized and codified was the product of evolution; but neither their cotemporaries nor posterity lost sight of that fact and that principle. Therefore the evolution continued. Although that literature of the *Tana'im* was accepted and indorsed by their successors, the *Amoraim* of Palestine and Babylon, as the established authority, the latter claimed the right to comparative criticism, to establish laws and precepts, and to enact new ones to meet new emergencies. The underlying principle of perpetual development could not be stopped by any written literature. And so the schools and courts of law as well as the synagogue produced commentaries to the rabbinical material converted into books, and these commentaries were called *Gemara*, "the finishing," that which settles finally the law, precept or custom, and points out their roots and origin in the Bible. In course of time, however, the commentaries became much larger and more important than the main matter. It was also supposed that the matter had been exhausted. The schools and academies declined in Palestine through the government of Christian emperors and the continuous emigration in consequence thereof; and in Babylon on account of the counter-pressure of Parseeism against Christianity, which bore heavily also upon the Jews. It was apprehended that "The Law will be forgotten," and the rabbis began again to compile systematically in their own way, both in Palestine and Babylon. The *Mishna* was taken as the main text, and the commentaries were added to each paragraph thereof, together with such other ethical, religious, historical and scientific fragments as the compilers considered worth preserving. Toward the end of the fourth century the compilation was closed in Palestine, and it is called the TALMUD YERUSHALMI or also the "Gemara of the West." Toward the end of the fifth century the compilation of the Babylonian rabbis was closed and called the TALMUD BABLI. Other works, especially of a homiletic nature, called *Midrashim*, and established rituals were added, always under the impression that the Talmud and Midrashim would establish forever the forms and methods of Judaism.

Centuries of stability followed. The heads of Judaism, men of undoubted authority, resided in Babylon. They were called *Saburaim* in the sixth century, and then *Gueonim* down to the end of the tenth century. They were holy men, learned in the Law. They decided all questions according to the Talmud for the Jews of Asia, Africa and Europe, and their decisions were laws for all Israel. The whole system was apparently immovable. The Talmud reigned by its expounders. Under that surface, however, the law of evolution continued its work. The study of philosophy, science and Grecian literature among the Arabs had its prominent apostles among the Jews. Unexpectedly there arose among the Jews the sect of the Karaites, who rejected the authority of the Talmud altogether, and among the orthodox new lights arose and culminated at last in the unexpected fact that one of the *Gueonim*, Saadiah of Fiuma, sanctioned the study of philosophy, and wrote a book on the subject. This was again the beginning of a new period. The office of the *Gueonim* was abrogated. The center of Judaism shifted from Asia into Europe, especially Spain, France and Germany, and the forms and methods changed once more.

In Spain, under the sway of the Mohammedans, a new and vigorous spirit broke through the forms and methods and built up that philosophical Judaism which, always remaining upon the ancient basis of the Sinaic revelation, produced on the one hand modern Judaism and influenced Christianity on the other hand, preparing its students for the Reformation. Those Spanish Jews were not only faithful believers in the Sinaic revelation, but also systematic philosophers, scientists, stern critics and honest men beyond the reach of Pope and Council and outside the magic circle of rabbinical and traditional forms and methods. While some of the greatest among them, together with the French and German rabbis, cultivated the Talmudical literature orthodoxly and commented and expounded, criticised and codified the Talmud with more scientific skill than those of Babylon exercised; many were engaged in expounding Judaism from the philosophical standpoint and leading it onward to new forms and methods.

Before we close this lecture on the Judaism of history—I can not exhaust the subject in one lecture—let us look back upon the change of standpoint in various ages. Moses gave form and method to the substance of the Sinaic revelation in State and Church, as it is called now. The form was broken in the time of Samuel, when Saul was elected King of Israel, for the King has no place in the laws of Moses. Whatever refers to a king in those laws is certainly of much later origin. The methods were changed by the Prophets, who insisted upon the spiritual and ethical contents of the Law, and attached no importance to the observances and ceremonies. When the Israelites were in captivity they did not observe the ceremonial laws of Moses, although they adhered steadfastly to the Sinaic revelation, the covenant and the promises. When they returned to Palestine the Mosaic law was never introduced in all its parts, although Ezra and Nehemiah insisted upon organizing the Second Commonwealth on the same basis as the first. During the existence of the Second Commonwealth an entirely new Thorah was developed, which found its expression in the Mishnah. From the very beginning up to this point, there was no stability; there was perpetual change and evolution of forms and methods. Unchanged and unchangeable in this perpetual fluctuation was only the Sinaic revelation, the covenant. This remained the same forever. Whatever the rabbis of the Talmud and their successors in Babylon did enact, introduce, write and enforce, did not change an iota of the Sinaic revelation and the covenant, although it did change laws and customs, forms and methods, replaced the old by new successors, always, however, in the same spirit and from the same standpoint that all laws, customs and observances are subject to change, because they are mere forms and methods, however holy, useful and beneficial they may be at this or that time or place; eternal and fixed is the word and covenant of God alone, and both are in the Sinaic revelation. Among the mistakes which those *Tana'im* made—every age makes its mistakes, or else the successors could find nothing to improve—was that they compiled and imposed every law, custom and observance upon the house of Israel under the impression that the nation, with all its peculiarities and elements, must be preserved, to be politically restored, which they expected to come to pass at once or in a very short time by a Messiah, or otherwise. This made their code too political and too large, so that the religious and ethical elements are almost hidden under the mountain of political laws. The Christian writers dropped the political element altogether, and attended to the religious and ethical exclusively; therefore, the New Testament, which in fact contains no more of it, spread more rapidly than the rabbinical writings. This mistake maintained its hold upon the Judaism of history, and still adheres to its orthodoxy. The Spanish school of Jewish reasoners began to correct that mistake, and thus became the source and starting-point of modern Judaism, as I expect to explain in my next lecture, to which you are respectfully invited.

XVII.
JUDAISM OF HISTORY.—PART II.

Rabbinical Judaism is that religious system which, on the basis of the material developed during the Second Commonwealth of the Hebrews, was built up by the various rabbis between the first and tenth Christian centuries, called *Ta'naim* to the end of the second century, *Amora'im* to the end of the fifth century, *Sabura'im* in the sixth century and *Gue'onim* to the end of the tenth century.

With all the piety, patriotism, learning, sagacity and profound morality of those various patristic teachers, they made notably two mistakes. (1) They considered every law of Moses eternally obligatory upon every Israelite; but most of those laws not being applicable under the emergencies of various ages, they were explained in a manner to meet those emergencies. Those decisions again being law, further decisions were again based upon those secondary laws, so that the body of laws became enormous, and in many instances obscured the laws of Moses, from which it was supposed to be derived. (2) They were too scrupulous with the inherited customs, disciplines and laws, so that every possible detail and doubt in the written and oral law was anxiously investigated, discussed and fixed, which enormously increased the body of rabbinical law. It took a man a lifetime to learn the whole law and carry it into practice.

The cause of all this was, in the first place, their scrupulously conscientious desire to live exactly according to the laws of Moses and the rabbis; and in the second place, their reserved right, wherever they lived, to be governed by their own laws, in the Roman Empire as well as in Persia, Spain, France, Germany and elsewhere. This exercised an excellent influence upon the Jewish mind, which was trained by the study of the Law, while others studied and learned nothing besides legends and hob-goblin stories, and made them conscientious, while knights and princes attended to their feuds, fights, chases and the whipping of dogs, horses and peasants. The laws of the rabbis protected the Israelite against the corruption of lawlessness, which was then the general law, the feudal and decretal laws of the rulers of nations. The Talmud cultivated the Jew, when all other elements of culture were confined to a few *fraters* in some convents, and a few scholasts carefully hiding their opinions behind the barriers of bad Latin.

Upon Judaism itself, as a religion, it had the evil effect that it distracted the attention of rabbis and laymen from the spirit and essence of religion and ethics, and captivated it in the mass of forms, observances and laws, which imposed upon it the outward appearance of "no religion." The Jew was a firm believer, a sound thinker in the Law, but he was no reasoner, he had no philosophy of religion. This was certainly injurious to his intelligence.

The combat against this evil was opened by the Gaon Saadia of Fiuma, in Egypt, and was continued by the Jewish philosophers of the Spanish school in Spain and Southern France, in Northern Africa and Western Asia, by prominent reasoners and scientists, especially physicians and astronomers who were well versed also in rabbinical lore, down to the expulsion of the Jews from Spain in the year 1492. The principal teachers and authors were Solomon Ibn Gabirol, who was the Vicebron of the Christian students; Bachia Ibn Pakudah, the moral philosopher; Abraham Ibn Daud, Judah Halevi, Abraham and Moses Ibn Ezra, Ibn Zadik, and the Ibn Thibbon family, all of whom were the forerunners of Moses Maimonides, who gave to the Jews not only his complete rabbinical code, *Mishnah Thorah*, and a large number of rabbinical commentaries, philosophical and medical writings, but also the first complete philosophy of religion in the three volumes of his *Moreh Nebuchim*, from which Jews, Christians and Mohammedans have adopted much for the advancement of rational religion. He was the great harmonizer of reason and faith. His successors were Gersonides, Creskas (opponent), Joseph Albo, Shem Tob Palquira, Isaac Arama, Samuel Sarsa, Isaac Abarbanel, and a host of others who made the philosophy of Judaism their particular study, and spread it by Hebrew translations (most of them wrote in Arabic) far and wide among the Jews of the civilized world, and by Latin translations among Christian students, although that Harvard College professor who lately wrote a text-book on Judaism knows nothing about it. Those philosophers wrote also critical commentaries on the Bible, especially Abraham Ibn Ezra, Levi Gersonides and Isaac Abarbanel, commentaries which, in many instances, revolutionized the old conceptions of the Bible, opened a new path to reasoners, and are still indispensable to Bible critics.

The new spirit cultivated by those philosophers and their cotemporaries gave rise to three phases of Judaism. 1. The historical or rabbinical Judaism which found its literature in the casuists and expounders of the Talmud mostly among the Spanish scholars and authors, like Alfasi and his disciples, Maimonides and his disciples, Nachmanides, Rabbi Asher (German) and his sons, Adereth and others, and the Franco-Germanic school of Rabbi Solomon ben Isaac or *Rashi*, who expounded and codified systematically the rabbinical material. It was again a new form of Judaism which they sought to establish and crystalize it forever. But they could not stop the law of evolution, and so there came behind them another corps of expounders and codifiers whose labors culminated in the sixteenth century in the Palestinean Joseph Caro, in the Polish Moses Isserls, who were again succeeded by others, perhaps of no less importance to Rabbinical Judaism, up to the very noonday of the nineteenth century. In the form of worship they went apart in the principal rituals with different shadings in each, viz: the Portuguese or *Sephardic*, the Germanic or *Minhag Ashkenaz*, and the Polish or *Minhag Polen*.

2. The Kabbalistic Judaism now called the *Chassidism*. Mysticism always follows in the wake of rationalism. The philosopher endeavors to explain everything, God, world, man, their relations, eternity and its mysteries, in which he can not possibly succeed to the satisfaction of all men. He exhausts himself and finally arrives at an inexplicable residue, which gives rise to mysticism in the unsatisfied minds. This is a law of history, and was also the case in Spain. Philosophy produced among its opponents that mysticism in religion and expounding of the Bible which is called the Kabbalah, and has its main literature in the *Zohar*, an extensive commentary to the five books of Moses, written in Spain, published and studied most extensively by Christians of the sixteenth century in Italy and Germany. This remarkable compendium of mysticism and poetry, truth and fiction, gave rise to a new literature among Jews and Christians, which at last culminated in the practical Kabbalah, especially in the Orient, in Russia and Poland, among pretending Messiahs, and among the so-called *Chassidim*, who are most numerous now in Russia, Galicia and Hungary. Their rabbis still converse with the angels, banish evil spirits, cure diseases by amulets and magic spells, are saints and workers of miracles. They are rabbinical Jews to a certain extent only. The *Zohar* is their holy book, and the rabbi their highest authority. Wherever this authority and that book collides with the Talmud and its casuists, or even with the laws of Moses, they follow their own established authority. Their ritual and form of worship are peculiar to themselves. In this point the Palestinean Rabbi, Isaac Luria, is their principal authority. Notwithstanding the fierce opposition of the orthodox rabbis to Kabbalism, many of the opinions, views, prayers, formulas and observances of the Kabbalists found their way into the later rabbinical literature, the orthodox liturgy and ritual, and became to the opposite side one of the main causes of reforms in the synagogue.

3. The philosophical or rational Judaism, whose main literature was also the Bible and the Talmud, differently expounded, however. The traditional

methods and forms were not considered the highest authority, from which there was no appeal to reason or science; free research and free thought took the places of traditional beliefs and rabbinical laws, Talmudical or post-Talmudical. The same relations of Judaism to the Talmud as the relations of Protestants to the Fathers and traditions of the Church were gradually established. The Jewish beliefs and doctrines, as expounded in that Spanish school, were placed conspicuously in front, the observances and rabbinical laws were placed in the background; reason, science and the progress of ages were allowed a large share in forming the religious opinion. The school of reasoners from Saadia down to Abarbanel became, by common consent, the authority.

The Jews driven from Spain, persecuted in Germany, and oppressed everywhere else, except in Holland and Belgium, driven in large numbers to the Orient, into Russia and Poland, outside of the progressive culture of Western Europe, fell back into an unreasoning orthodoxy, as oppressed and persecuted people always do, and built up that rabbinism and kabbalism, under which the masses are still held spellbound, as are the Mohammedans, Greek and Roman Catholics of the same regions. Overawed and terrified by priests, princes and mobs, deprived of the freedom of speech, pressed into narrow ghettoes, ridiculed by petulant writers and travestied by comedians, the Jew was silent, dumfounded, and would not utter a rational idea, fearing it might be offensive to the Church or the State. Not entirely, however, were the Jews silent. Even in Poland, where Rabbi Lipmann had written his *Nizzachon*, a rational commentary on the Bible, against the accepted Christian and Jewish exegesis, in grateful recognition of which he was burnt alive by the holy men of the Church; even in Poland Isaac Troki wrote his *Chizzak Emunah* in the same spirit as the *Nizzachon*, and Rabbi Lipman Heller stood at the head of the Polish rabbis, although his commentaries to the Mishnah were more scientific than orthodox. Germany produced quite a number of reasoners and scientists. Spinoza wrote in Holland, and the Jewish culture culminated in Italy, where the disciples of Maimonides and Abraham Ibn Ezra were quite numerous, and figured as professors of universities, teachers of cardinals and princes, and physicians of popes as well as of sultans and emperors. The number of enlightened and progressive men like Sepurno, Elias Levita, Azariah dei Rossi, Leon di Modena, the Del Medigos, the historiographer Gans, and the reformatory, though anti-philosophical, Rabbi Jacob Emden, was not very small. The masses of the Hebrew people, living under continuous oppression and constant fear of the Church authorities, remained orthodox, silent and exclusive. The humane and enlightened eighteenth century encouraged also the Jew and brought him out of his dark retreats. The zephyr of spring moved the minds in the ghettoes, and men of distinction, of mind and learning ventured out into broad daylight. Moses Mendelssohn was the representative man of the age. That timid philosopher, the author of *Phædan* and *Morgenstunden*, the translator of the Pentateuch, Psalms and Ecclesiastes and commentator of several books of the Bible, became a conductor of modern culture to his people and a representative expounder of Judaism to his many Christian friends and opponents. New forms and methods were developed among the Jews, in Germany especially. The spirit of the Spanish school resurrected in Germany. The French Revolution, the succeeding wars, then the reaction and the new despotism in Germany and Austria kept that spirit at bay and smothered every reformatory movement. Then came the struggle for emancipation and captivated the minds; it retarded, but it could not stop the law of evolution, which went on under the surface. It culminated first in a new Jewish literature of history, criticism, theology and its branches; and then in a spirit of reformation, which found its expression in a number of rabbinical conferences, in which the Spanish school, in connection with German learning and culture, declared its triumphs over the rabbinical and Kabbalistic orthodoxy.

So the newest phase of Judaism was begotten. It re-echoes in Italy, France and England. It celebrates its triumphs in Hungary, Poland and Russia. It was carried into the United States of America, where in the short period of one generation it was transformed into American Judaism. Nowhere in all Europe could that reformatory spirit manifest itself in its full vigor. Old and stereotyped forms and institutions, the orthodoxy of princes and priests, together with the intolerance of nations and the fanaticism of the masses, were and are now indestructible barriers, insurmountable obstacles. Emancipation and then the preservation of the recaptured rights of man, together with the domineering materialism, atheism and hatred against religion which characterized almost all European Democrats, turned ever so many excellent minds from Judaism and checked the reformatory spirit. In this country, however, where the forms and institutions of Judaism had to be newly established, perfect freedom reigned in the government and people, and the number of sects is so large that the mutual prejudices could be but very mild; here in this blessed country that reformatory spirit which, for centuries, had been the undercurrent of the apparently defunct and benumbed forms of Judaism, triumphed in practical institutions, new forms and methods, as it did nowhere in the world; and from here it reacts on Europe as do our political institutions. American Judaism is, in forms and methods, far ahead of the Jewish congregations in any and every other country, Germany not excepted. Practically the spirit of the Spanish school resurrects in the American Judaism, with its love of freedom, its spirit of charity and benevolence, humanism and fraternization, its patriotic principles and national attachment, its *Minhag America* and its American spirit of progress and unification. Let those Spanish Hidalgoes of the Jewish mind rise and see how they live anew in American Judaism.

And yet what is the fundamental principle of all those changes in form and method? It is in the first place the Sinaic revelation, the covenant of God and Israel, with its eternal doctrines and laws, precepts and ordinances, which man has not made and man can not change. Under all the revolutions and changes of thirty-four centuries of history, this basis was not changed, not touched even; this standpoint was not affected by the law of evolution. It was, is, and will remain forever the immovable corner-stone of Israel's and mankind's positive religion. Necessity, the pressure of events, reduced it to Palestinean religion, Babylonian and Egyptian religion, Roman and German or Spanish religion, tribal religion, ghetto religion, rabbinical or Kabbalistic. But all these changed forms and methods are the offspring of evolution and outer circumstances, the children of time fluctuating and transitory, and the fundamental principle of the Sinaic revelation and the covenant remain unchanged forever.

And in the second place it is the principle of reform, progress, change of forms and methods which underlies the whole process of Jewish history. The mobility of stability is its chief characteristic. The immovable center is the Sinaic revelation and the covenant. All from center to surface is subject to perpetual metamorphosis. The sound and vigorous center imparts perpetual life and movement to all parts of that sphere, and compels the perpetual changes of form and method, in order to remain in correspondence with the surroundings of the outer world.

Proceed, go on, always onward and forward, benign spirit of progress and advancement, with reason's aid, the advice of goodness, and with Heaven's voice: "I, Jehovah, am thy *Elohim*." Go on and unite all good men in peace and harmony, for the blessing and happiness of man, and to the glory of God and His eternal word.

XVIII.
THE CHRISTIANITY OF HISTORY.

It is not right, perhaps, that I write a lecture on the Christianity of history, as I do not comprehend and understand Christianity as a Christian would; and I know, on the other hand, that Christians like Hitzig, Kuenen, Wellhausen, or also Millman and that learned professor of Harvard College, writing on the Judaism of history, make very considerable mistakes, partly by their ignorance of the Jewish literature and partly by the misunderstanding of the spirit and essence of that literature and the people that produced it. I will, therefore, be brief and cautious in my remarks on this important subject.

It is admitted on all sides that Christianity in its primitive and original form was a Jewish sect, and so remained for a very long time in the Orient, so that the Romans for many years knew no difference between Jew and Christian, although Paul, the Apostle to the Gentiles, declared the Law abrogated. If this is so, it must also be true that primitive Christianity no less than Judaism based itself upon the Sinaic revelation and adhered also to the laws of Moses, which were read in the churches as well as the synagogues, until the Emperor Hadrian prohibited this ancient practice. Then the Gospel according to Mark was written to be read among the Nazarenes of Jerusalem instead of the Law and the Prophets. But long after that the Oriental Christians lived according to the laws of Moses, until at last they were excommunicated by the Gentile Christians. Paul's protestations against the law and circumcision were in nowise directed against the Sinaic revelation and covenant, although he goes back to the Abrahamitic covenant; for he preached the same moral doctrine and the same God, who should be again "all in all," when the Son will return the kingdom to the Father. He held so firmly to the laws of the Decalogue that he commanded the adulterer among his flock to be put to death; and claimed that the covenant had been inherited by the Gentiles. The abolition of the law referred to the political, civil, criminal, ceremonial or Levitical laws, all that concerned the State, the temple, the altar, the sacrifices, the priesthood; not to the moral law and the religious doctrine. This, I believe, is admitted by the orthodox expounders of the New Testament. Hence it must also be admitted that the Sinaic revelation and the covenant were the fundamental principle of primitive and original Christianity, and the protestations of its founders were directed only against a portion of the laws and institutions of Moses and what was based upon them by Sanhedrin, scribes and popular customs, observances and opinions. Therefore reformation in Christendom actually signifies returning to the standpoint and basis of the Sinaic revelation and the covenant for the entire human family.

The abrogation of those laws was necessary for the promulgation of Christianity. The political laws of the Jews with their theocratic and democratic foundation, especially after the fall of Jerusalem, were an abomination to the Romans and Greeks. The sacrificial polity was not only impracticable outside of Palestine, but it had been outlived, as is evident from Jewish written sources. The Hebrews themselves had already established a new form of worship in the numerous cities in Palestine, Egypt, Persia and elsewhere. Christianity, in order to succeed among the Gentiles, had to appear among them without those laws and circumcision, only with the Sinaic revelation and the covenant as understood and expounded by the Prophets, and as accepted by those "devout Gentiles" of whom Paul speaks so often.*

Christianity, starting out without laws, made its Talmud entirely different from that of the Jews, although it was developed by the same law of evolution as Judaism was. It made, in course of time, a Talmud of Rome, a Talmud of Constantinople, and at last a Talmud of Protestanism. With the laws of Moses, also the freedom, equality and stern justice underlying them were relinquished, abandoned to the so-called wordly rulers, which was a great loss to humanity. The Church had nothing to do with the laws. It dealt in doctrines which were crystallized into dogmas and creeds, in disciplines which were fixed and enforced, and in church property which was accumulated and governed. Although the patristic writers of the Church, whether dogmatic, homiletic, exegetic, legendary or epistolary, strictly adhered to the rabbinical method, the *Derashah*, which means expounding Scriptures without established rules of interpretation, to advance doctrines and precepts deemed necessary or requisite for the instruction or edification of the masses; they did not discuss law or *Halachah* as the rabbis did; hence the Christian Talmud became dogmatic and purely speculative, under the guidance of Greco-Alexandrian or Greco-Roman methods with some, and without any logic or system with others.

The difficulties which they had to overcome were numerous. They had inherited the Jewish and the Gentile Christianity, with the law and without it, with Jewish opinions and Pagan fragments; the Jewish Messiah and

---

*For a more extensive exposition of these points see the author's "Lectures on the Origin of Christianity."

second advent belief of the original Apostles, the *Metathronic* Son of God, the end of the world, and the last judgment day at hand, in the teachings of Paul, the *Logos* mystery and of the Alexandrian school in the Gospel according to John, the Holy Ghost theories of Jewish mystics, and the plurality of deities in the Heathen consciousness; the different natures and offices of their Messiah and the various accounts of his conception, birth, genealogy, life, death, resurrection and ascension. All these difficulties and contradictions they were called upon to overcome, harmonize and crystallize into a dogmatic Christology, which certainly was no small piece of work and no common incentive to the mind for the exercise of ingenuity and reasoning powers, in dealing with abstract questions, and reducing a chain of thoughts into the stereotyped words of a dogma

This form of mental labor was certainly beneficial. It made the Christian teachers idealistic, while the Jewish rabbis remained realistic up to the days of the Spanish school. Its nugatory influence was, that it absorbed the mind by one field of human speculation to the detriment of all others. Practical life with all its important questions were excluded from the student's sphere. He was a theologian, and naturally attempted to make all persons and things theological or useless. The mind concentrated on dogmatic speculations, became one-sided, intolerant and fanatical, which caused the endless feuds and quarrels in the Church; the persecution, oppression and frequent slaughter of so-called heretics, schismatics and infidels; and the relentless combats of priests, princes and nations on account of dogmas, which one believed and the other denied. The large masses of people unable to reason with the dogmatists, understood nothing of the theological questions, remained ignorant and helpless tools in the hands of the priests, who succeeded easily in making them believe anything they pleased. The people remained as ignorant of the affairs of the Church as they did of the affairs of the State. They were governed soul and body. The reasoners, too, were gradually reduced to a method of reasoning from imaginary premises without any reference to facts, phenomena and realities, so that they became mere advocates of the domineering system without the energy to rise above it and survey it from another standpoint.

To this mental and spiritual state of affairs another factor must be added; this was the constantly growing wealth and power of the Church, its servants and devotees. This naturally gave rise to Church legislation by potentates on the one hand, by Pope and Council, or also by inferior prelates on the other, to establish and protect the Church, the orthodox dogmas and fixed disciplines, the priesthood and the domains of the Church; a legislation which grew into the Canon Law, by which Christendom has been governed and is governed to-day, with or without the consent of the nations or the individuals thereof. This ecclesiastical power and dominion had certainly its beneficial influence. The Canon Law was by far better than none, and there was none among the domineering ruffians of knights and chivalric princes who despised knowledge as they did labor and the laborer, and recognized only the right of might. The ecclesiastical power counterpoised the lawless power of despots for the benefit of the governed masses. It gave to students a material aside from the dogmatic quibbling in which they were ingulfed. Notwithstanding the horrible wrongs sanctioned or instigated by Church legislation, the burning of infidels, witches and lunatics; the persecution and oppression of Jews and Turks; the absolution for rich sinners and the slavery imposed upon the helpless multitude; notwithstanding all that and much more, the Canon law was a holy thing, a piece of divinity in the minds of the masses, the reasoner and the thoughtless, priest or layman, exactly as the Talmud was to the Jew and the tradition to the Mohammedan.*

This is the organism which the law of evolution brought forth in the Church. This is the variety of forms and methods which rose and disappeared or remained in Christendom. This is the material of which the Talmud of Rome and the Talmud of Constantinople and St. Petersburg are composed, with all the wisdom and follies, truth and fiction, kindness and cruelty, justice and bloody wrongs, which they contain; all to establish a Christology which they might be pleased to call orthodox, a church and priesthood to protect and promulgate that very Christology, a form of worship with a form of domination. It was a colossal aparatus to lift a fly, a furious Vesuvius to roast an egg, much ado about nothing. The whole noise was about the different reports concerning Jews which had reached the patristic writers, the clashing contradictions which that produced, and the quarrels of priests over it. The starting point, primitive and original Christianity according to either Peter, Paul or John, was lost sight of; the Sinaic revelation and the covenant were almost forgotten, and the whole affair was forced upon another field, the field of Christology "which thy fathers knew not." The revealed matter, that which is acknowledged on all sides as revealed matter, was laid aside; and the specula-

---

*In Austria and Germany the Talmud has lately been attacked quite severely by Christian professors, and defended by the rabbis. But none of them has had the moral courage to advance that there is certainly no absurdity in the Talmud which is not duplicated in the dogmatic discussions, and no injustice which is not outdone by some canon law of the Church, or some decree of a Council. And yet such is the recorded fact.

tion and legislation of priests was taken up in its stead. The servant occupies the master's chair.

And now comes Protestanism. Huss protested. Luther, Melanchthon, Calvin and Zwingly protested. Erasmus, of Amsterdam, Vander Houghton, Henry VIII., of England, and Gustavus Adolphus, of Sweden, protested, and they found numerous followers who declared that the old form of Christianity had been broken, the scholastic methods had outlived their days of usefulness. The men of the fifteenth and sixteenth centuries began a new chapter of history by the invention of typography, the revival of letters, the establishment of commerce, the remodeling of state governments, the cultivation of philosophy, the study of the classical remains of antiquity. The minds were no longer ingulfed in dogmatic theology exclusively; it was no longer all-important. Other themes engaged the minds, and a spirit of freedom appeared on the horizon of man which penetrated into the churches and convents, rousing some monks, priests and scholiasts to recognize and do justice to that new spirit which traveled through the nations of Western Europe. It is hard to decide whether those reformers or their cotemporaries were unfit for a thorough reformation; but it is certain that while they reformed disciplines and pretended to reject the whole Talmud of Rome with all its traditions, dogmatism and canon law, they advanced the old orthodoxy in a new form without any attempt to come back to primitive and original Christianity. They not only retained the whole burden of Christology as established by Popes and Councils, but made it so much more oppressive to the mind, by denying the right of reason and negativing the existence of free will altogether, making of the Bible a new and infallible Pope, and of their Christology the indispensable chariot in which to ride into Heaven. A new Talmud was gradually evolved from the defunct remains of the old, the Talmud of Protestantism. Those good men then certainly believed they had fixed and secured forever their special form and method of religion, never to be disturbed again. They forgot the law of evolution. They forgot that they disturbed one system, and whatever disturbs can be disturbed.

In spite of Christian theology and churchcraft the European nations advanced from the darkness of the Middle Ages to the morning dawn of the sixteenth century. 'So also, in spite of all the blunders made in the Reformation, the European nations advanced from the dawn in the sixteenth century to the high noon of the nineteenth. Pressed onward by the spread of science, commerce, industry and enlightenment to the revolutions of the eighteenth century in all provinces of human activity, Christianity against its will was also revolutionized. The old Christology of supposed facts was changed into a speculative Christology, by men like

Frederick Schleiermacher, Kant, Schelling, Hegel, the English theists, the Saxon Unitarians of Transylvania, and a host of other men and societies, who wanted to be Christians by name at least. For that speculative or rational Christology means a negation of supposed facts, in place of which the idea is set. They do not maintain apodictically that the alleged facts are not true; they only consider them indifferent and superfluous. The ideas which they represent are sufficient to constitute a satisfactory Christology; anyhow they are amply sufficient to show why the Christian world always believed those allegations to be historical facts and to confer upon their churches, sects or societies the title of Christian. This is the last phase of Christian reformation; the next step beyond leads into the Sinaic revelation and the covenant as the sole foundation of positive religion.

Those men, Schelling and Hegel included, make one great mistake, which has the effect of keeping many in a vicious circle, of the same nature precisely as that of the orthodox dogmatics, when they proved their dogmas by some accidental statement in the New Testament or also in the Old as understood by some prior dogmatists. Those modern doctors who care not about facts, tell us the New Testament Scriptures were a mere and imperfect beginning of Christianity, giving the impulse to a new development, in which each succeeding stage is superior to the preceding one, so that the modern Unitarian stands upon the top of the ladder. Christianity in its historical development and progress of Christian thought, has left its sects from every phase of development as a sort of documentary history, which proves beyond a doubt that each succeeding sect is more enlightened than the preceding.

It is not very likely that those very sects will admit this allegation. But suppose this be admitted, it merely proves that Christian thinkers were and are now engaged in undoing what their predecessors have built up. It is a process of self-destruction, or, at least, of destroying all Christology. Those modern gentlemen actually maintain that Christology based on fact is no longer tenable, and they adopt instead the conglomeration of ideas, which they call rational Christology. Why do they catch the shadows when the substance is evaporated? Because, they say, the Christian mind which historically developed those dogmas, must necessarily possess the ideas which it incarnated in supposed facts; therefore we must necessarily build up a speculative Christology. But the Christian mind at no time dealt with ideals, it received a number of traditions concerning the Messiah, his natures, offices and teachings, verily believed to be facts without any reference to any idea. So the acts and lessons of the Apostles were again received as facts and not as a presentation of ideas. All that Christian students did in this direction was to harmonize those contradictory traditions and cast them into dogmas, which the populace believed and the philosophers attempted to expound. But if those traditions are not facts, where is the necessity of harmonizing them, hence where is the substance, the truth or the necessity of that so-called rational Christology?

If they maintain that they must stop somewhere, at some standing-point from which to develop a system of Christianity, therefore, they stop at the ideas incorporated in the orthodox Christology, as the legacy of the past, upon which the present state of the popular mind is based; they tell the truth, but must admit at the same time that the popular mind being taken away from those facts to the ideas thereof, will necessarily be prepared to drop the ideas as well as the facts, which will be the end of that so-called rational Christology. What will remain then? Either the return into the mediæval dogmatic speculations in alleged facts, or a simple return to the Sinaic revelation and the covenant, the standpoint upon which Jesus and his Apostles stood together with the primitive Christians, or atheism and immorality, if the philosophers do not succeed better in the future than they did in the past by giving us a Living God and a living moral law, living and enlivening, convincing and assuring. The law of evolution can make no positive religion.

If the last phases of Christian reformation offer correct material from which to predict the future, we know exactly the creed of the future man. In the past it was not the Talmud of the Jews nor the Talmud of the Christians, nor the wrangling of the reformers against both of them, nor any other phase, form or method which the law of evolution produced, that advanced the human family from crude and childish notions of God and His will to our present conceptions of both. It was neither Rabbinism and Kabbalism nor the Christology of the orthodox or the dissenters, all of which were mere means to lead man to God and human duty, which civilized and humanized the masses. It was the substance of the Sinaic revelation as the acknowledged law of God, and the consciousness of His covenant of love with His children, which was spread by these or those means; it was that and nothing else which elevated man to the dignity of a child of God, and pointed out for him the path leading to the Father's house. This revelation and this covenant, spread by those and other means, were the redeeming power in Christendom. The means are the form. It is broken. The essence remains. On this platform we meet again. "The grass withereth, the flower fadeth, and the word of our God lasteth forever."

THE END.

CONTENTS.

NO OF LECTURE.		PAGE.
I.	AGREEMENTS,	3
II.	INSPIRATION, PROPHECY AND REVELATION,	10
III.	PROPHECY, REVELATION AND THE BIBLE,	16
IV.	THE JEWISH AND THE CHRISTIAN EVIDENCES OF REVELATION COMPARED,	23
V.	THE LAWS OF MOSES AND THE LAWS OF PROGRESS,	28
VI.	THE HIGHEST AUTHORITY AFTER REVELATION,	35
VII.	SINAI AND CALVARY COMPARED FROM THE ETHICAL STANDPOINT,	42
VIII.	FREEDOM, THE POSTULATE OF ETHICS,	49
IX.	PROVIDENCE AND THE DOGMA,	56
X.	SIN AND ATONEMENT,	63
XI.	IMMORTALITY AND SINAI,	70
XII.	A RESUME OF THE BODY OF THE DOCTRINE,	77
XIII.	PARADISE, HELL, SATAN, EVIL SPIRITS OR RECOMPENSE,	84
XIV.	I.—GIFTS OF GRACE, REDEMPTION AND SALVATION,	91
XV.	II.—GIFTS OF GRACE, REDEMPTION AND SALVATION,	98
XVI.	I.—THE JUDAISM OF HISTORY,	104
XVII.	II.—THE JUDAISM OF HISTORY,	111
XVIII.	THE CHRISTIANITY OF HISTORY,	117

www.ingramcontent.com/pod-product-compliance
Lightning Source LLC
Chambersburg PA
CBHW020122170426
43199CB00009B/597